Michael Bruce Ross And Other Killers

James Bird

Published by Trellis Publishing, 2021.

While every precaution has been taken in the preparation of this book, the publisher assumes no responsibility for errors or omissions, or for damages resulting from the use of the information contained herein.

MICHAEL BRUCE ROSS AND OTHER KILLERS

First edition. July 1, 2021.

Copyright © 2021 James Bird.

ISBN: 979-8224567478

Written by James Bird.

MICHAEL BRUCE ROSS AND OTHER KILLERS

JAMES BIRD

To Punish, To Help or To Learn?

'When I am finally executed, the vast majority of the people of this state will celebrate my death.' So wrote Michael Bruce Ross, murderer, rapist, stalker. Here, surely, is a man who deserves everything the state can throw at him. Yet when we examine his case, matters begin to seem more complicated than that.

Of the many, many criminals who end up on death row, Michael Ross's situation is one of the most complex. Some reluctant guests of the row are vicious and wicked; men and women filled with pure evil. Others are innocent. These are victims of a system which is far from fool proof and frequently driven by political expediency as much as a search for justice.

And some people are killers despite themselves, criminals in need of help as well as punishment. Ross fits comfortably into none of those categories. And that is what makes his case so interesting. There is no doubt that he committed murder; there is no doubt he committed rape. He admits as much himself. For that reason, this story needs also to be about his victims – the suffering they and their families endured goes beyond anything we feel for Ross. We should never forget that.

But this truth should not distract from the fact that Michael Ross's crimes, his arrest, his subsequent trial and ultimate execution are matters that should not be allowed to float away into the darkness. Yes, wickedness flowed from him, but his story is not that simple.

Ross was born in the small town of Putnam, Connecticut on July 26th 1959. He was brought up on a farm close to nearby Brooklyn. This part of New England sounds idyllic. The area bursts with wealth and history. It was home to Revolutionary War hero Israel Putnam (the town of Ross's birth was named after the General); in 1833 it saw the trial of Prudence Crandall – her crime was to have educated black children.

In other words, this part of Connecticut is renowned as a liberal, forward thinking area where justice is seen as an essential element of a well-run and fair society. As we shall see, in this respect the state seemed to suffer a momentary bout of forgetfulness when it came to the sordid case of Michael Ross.

The local population – which is overwhelmingly white – has plenty of employment. This is timber and farming country. Even today, in the age of technology, agriculture remains an important part of the economy. Indeed, Ross was brought up on a farm. He was a bright boy, successful in school. He was the eldest of four siblings, and loved to potter around the family farm helping his father, Daniel, when he got home from school, or through the long summer holidays.

On the face of it, then, it would seem that Ross had an idyllic upbringing. Unfortunately, that was not true. Daniel had married Patricia Laine as a matter of duty. She was already pregnant with Michael when they tied the knot. Theirs was not a happy relationship. Patricia was a highly unstable woman, with a depressive and difficult personality. Relations between husband and wife were rarely good.

Their farm produced chickens and eggs, and as such required constant work to keep on top of things. Under such pressure, Daniel and Pat fought pretty constantly. Frequently their arguments would turn physical. Both drank heavily, and there were rumours of drug abuse, although that was neither proven nor, to be fair, particularly worthy of note in the liberated days of the 1960s.

But the family's problems did not end there. Today, we would see in Patricia evidence of mental illness. Maybe it was something induced post pregnancy, or a trait inherent in her. Unfortunately, her capacity for the irrational and the violent were characteristics that would emerge in Michael as he began to grow up.

Patricia felt no pressure to internalise her struggles. She took a lot of her anger and confusion out on her children. Michael, as the eldest, bore the brunt of this. Mothers and sons are meant to share the strongest bonds, but they were largely missing in the Ross household.

This, and the probability that his mother's mental illness was inherited by Michael, could go a long way to explaining the confused, violent and deeply remorseful man that he became. But that is in the future. Eventually, life on the farm became too much for Pat. She formed a relationship with another man and ran away, headed for North Carolina. Quite what effect this had on the family we cannot be sure. Maybe, even, it was positive, because the source of much of the violence and conflict on the farm was removed.

The pressure on Daniel was immense, though. Despite being farmers, the Ross family was not wealthy, and suddenly Daniel had not only a farm to run, but four young children to look after. He turned to his eldest to become the support his wife had never quite been able to be. Michael has fond memories of helping out with the chores on the farm, and also of the responsibility of assisting his father. On the other hand the memories of the violence he suffered at the hands of his mother were closeted away, and the cupboard door firmly locked.

But experiences like these fester if not dealt with, and that would certainly seem to have been the case with the childhood years of this strange, troubled serial killer. In fact, the beatings he suffered only came to light when his sister revealed them; they were events to which he would not return, even when facing the death penalty.

Unsurprisingly Pat's North Carolina adventure did not work out. She returned to the family home, but her depressive thoughts of suicide, and open admission of beating her kids led to her being admitted to a mental health institution. The family would continue, effectively, with a single parent.

If Michael Ross put aside memories of the violence he suffered at the hands of his mother, then the same applied to abuse he experienced from another family member. His uncle was just a young man himself, not even out of his teens, when he sexually abused the boy he was meant to be babysitting.

In fact, that uncle eventually committed suicide, which may be more evidence of mental health problems passed down the family line. Children are strange beasts, and young Michael could well have blamed himself for his uncle's death. As the victim of the abuse which led to the perpetrator taking his own life, he could easily experience misplaced responsibility. The picture is emerging of a highly dysfunctional and, in many ways, tragic childhood which could not fail to have played a part in the man Michael Ross grew up to be.

One particular consequence of his mother's absence was that an unpleasant task fell to him. On a chicken farm, there are many birds who become sick, or are born malformed. It became the responsibility of Michael to deal with these unfortunate creatures. He would strangle them with his bare hands. Often, farmers have a more functional relationship with their animals than the wider population, but nevertheless violence towards animals is a common forerunner to violence against humans.

Michael's situation was slightly different to the norm, in that he was instructed to carry out these tasks, rather than choose to do them, but nevertheless, there must have been some impact on the development of empathy in the child – especially as he was given this responsibility when only eight years old.

All told, it is not excusable but is very understandable that by the time he entered high school, Ross was exhibiting highly anti-social behaviour. He was stalking young girls. Eventually, while still a very young man, he would be charged twice for related crimes He was a bright boy, with an IQ in the 120s, and coped well with his studies. But if intellectually intelligent, socially, he was anything but.

At the age of eighteen he won a place at Cornell University to study agricultural economics. He soon found himself in his first proper relationship, and dreamed of marrying the young woman with whom he had fallen in love. They even thought about marriage. But then the student fell pregnant, and decided on an abortion. That signalled the beginning of the end of the relationship. For the woman this was probably fortunate. Ross was beginning to realise that there was something within him that was not quite right. He began to have increasingly violent fantasies about his partner, always sexual in intent. It is not impossible that she would have become another of his victims.

This was the late seventies, and the idea that a man would seek help with such problems was unthinkable. This was a time when television and film was littered with sexual violence towards women. To treat women as objects rather than people was, it is sad to say, the norm. And so, rather than addressing the problems he was aware were growing inside of him, he allowed them to take hold.

Once more he became a stalker, and it was inevitable that it was only a matter of time before this escalated into physical and sexual violence. By his final year at Cornell he was engaged, but that did not stop his fantasies. He committed his first rape, then shortly afterwards, his first killing.

Dzung Ngoc Tu was a twenty five year old Cornell University student. When her body was found in a narrow creek deep in a steep sided valley fellow students and even University police initially thought that here was another tragic individual who had 'gorged out'. Suicides at the institution were, back in the early 1980s, too commonplace. A regular site for these terrible events was one of the two deep gorges, and the bridges that crossed them, close to the university.

However, those who knew her better realised that the quiet, attentive Vietnamese student was not a likely candidate for suicide. 'She was very quiet and unassuming is what I got from people she came and did her stuff and that was that,' recalled investigator Scott Hamilton.

Few knew much about Ross's first victim. It would be many years before her murderer would be discovered.

Seven months later, in early January 1982 Ross struck once more. This time, it was an attack much closer to his birthplace. Tammy Williams was killed in Brooklyn, Connecticut. She was just seventeen years old, and had simply been walking home from her boyfriend's house when she was attacked, raped, and strangled to death.

Justine Smith, a close friend, emphasised that Tammy and she were 'normal teenage girls.' They enjoyed playing pool, listening to music. They were starting to explore relationships with boyfriends. They loved to just hang out in that innocent, unthinking way that teenagers do. For Tammy, she would never move beyond that stage.

Justine thinks fondly of her friend: 'I can still remember the way she laughed. She had a heart of gold. I still remember her giggle, she was a fun person to be around,' she remembers.

In fact, the girls had gone to the same school as Ross, and often took shortcuts near his family farm.

Ross's offending began to escalate. Just two months had passed when he picked up Paula Perrera of Middletown, New York. She was even younger than Tammy Williams had been, just sixteen years old. By this point, Ross was working as a life insurance salesman, and that meant him travelling around a large area of the North Eastern part of the US.

Paula possessed a sense of adventure, a risk taking element which mixed with the innocence of her age. While that is not an unusual combination, it is a dangerous one. The teenager sought her thrills by hitching rides with strangers. And that innocence came to play in her belief that she was safe because she 'wouldn't accept rides from anyone creepy', as she told friends. Today, youngsters know that most predators are skilled enough to avoid looking 'creepy' – back in the 1980s, many kids saw threats as people dressed strangely, with twisted features as much as twisted minds. Ross was anything but that simplistic caricature of wickedness.

The intelligent, loquacious, well dressed, college educated man would appear as trustworthy to a naïve young girl as an elderly nun in a Nissan. Yet, soon he had stopped on a side road, raped her and killed her before calmly easing back onto Interstate 84 and driving on towards Connecticut.

An added element to this crime is that while Paula was just sixteen, she looked much younger. She enjoyed music from such innocents as Abba and the Monkeys; she danced to the Beach Boys. That innocence continued in her looks – her curly blond hair and blue eyes were enhanced by childish dimples. She stood just five feet tall. She would pass as twelve as much as sixteen. Still, Ross targeted her.

Just another couple of months passed before the killer struck again. This time on 15th June in Griswold, Connecticut. Debra Taylor was a victim of chance She and her husband had run out of gas, and had decided to split up to look for a gas station. Ross happened to pass her as she wandered by the side of the road, kidnapped her, then raped and strangled her. It was four months before her skeleton was found.

It seems as though Ross went quiet for a while following Debra's death. Perhaps he had experienced a shock. It certainly seems as though he fought hard – but unsuccessfully – against the demons inside of him. Then, in November 1983, nineteen year old Robin Stavinsky of Norwich, Connecticut, went missing. She had set out to go hitchhiking around her hometown. When she was discovered a week later, she had been raped and strangled.

Police finally began to spot a pattern. Like Tammy Williams and Debra Taylor, Robin was discovered face down, and had been sodomized. Her death was, as with the other victims, a result of strangulation.

On April 22nd, 1984 Ross struck twice, targeting his youngest victims. April Brunias and Leslie Shelley were just fourteen years old. They had taken themselves off to the movies and were walking over to a friend's house when Ross made his move. Detectives who found their bodies discovered crimes similar in nature to a number of others in the extended area. They were now certain that they had a serial killer on their hands.

The killings were, it seemed, especially brutal and heartless. The two girls had planned to get a lift home with the parent of their friend, but instead made the fatal and foolish decision to hitch hike. It is easy to imagine the youngsters daring each other to take the risk. They were unfortunate enough to be picked up by Ross. He drove them to a secluded spot, then ordered Leslie into the boot. He raped April and then strangled her before turning his attention to her friend. Who can bear to imagine the fear in their young minds as the danger they were in gradually dawned upon them?

On June 13th of the same year Ross struck for the final time. Wendy Baribeault was a seventeen year old who lived in Lisbon Connecticut. She was making her way to a convenience store on State Highway 12 when she was abducted by Ross. As with his other victims, Wendy was raped and strangled.

But this time a witness was found. A man with a blue Toyota had been observed following Wendy as she made her away along the road; a man who wore glasses. Ross wore spectacles, was in the area on the day in question and drove a blue Toyota; the police had their breakthrough.

Michael Bruce Ross's case is complex, because he is a complex person. As we shall see, the judiciary did not treat him well and there were many aspects to his personality which did not receive due attention at his trial, or the subsequent appeals. Nevertheless, he killed eight innocent young women and girls. He destroyed eight families. That point should never be forgotten. Sadly, it often is as people debate the rightness or otherwise of what happened to Ross next. The victims' stories fade, and begin to be lost. That is not right.

After Wendy Baribeault was discovered, Michael Malchik was the investigator put in charge of the case. Malchik was nothing if not thorough. He decided to interview a list of every blue Toyota owner living in the wider area. Given that Toyota is one of the most popular car brands in the world, and blue is anything but an unusual colour, this was no small undertaking.

Eventually, Malchik arrived at the door of a young salesman with a college education. Ross was living in Jewett City, a town in Connecticut close to Griswold. His responses to Malchik's questions give a clue to the mixed up man that he was. He quickly admits to having been arrested as a teen for sex offences. These were, as much as such things can ever be, minor, and had prompted no long term follow up or monitoring.

But was Ross's confession a clever move because he knew his actions would be on record? Or a deliberate attempt to get himself questioned further? It seems likely to have been the latter, because Malchik noted that Ross dropped several hints that the police might have found their man. The investigator decided that the conversation should continue at the station, and Ross was happy enough to oblige.

There, in the cold and formal setting of the police headquarters, Ross chatted away to Malchik like he was speaking to an old school friend. He discussed family – his parents were now divorced and the farm sold - girlfriends and gossiped about life in general. And, by the by, he confessed to the murder and kidnapping of eight young women, and the rape of seven of them.

An open and shut case. Yes, in terms of whether or not Ross was the culprit behind the crimes. But not in terms of the psychology of the man which led him to such abhorrent acts. There are those who, quite understandably, look at his victims and his crimes, and conclude that Ross deserved to die. There are others who realise that Ross was a very troubled man; although he can never again be allowed to set foot in the free world, maybe experts could learn from him and prevent other killings in the future. A touch of short term compassion might lead in the long term to the saving of other lives through the early detection and treatment of potential sexual and serial killers.

Somewhat sadly, his legal team attempted a technical defense against two of the murders, that of the youngest victims April and Leslie. They had not been murdered in Connecticut, argued the lawyers, and therefore it did not fall within the remit of the state to try Ross for their deaths. The whole question of where the actual murders occurred was open to debate, but the state successfully argued that in any case the crime had begun in Connecticut, and therefore did fall under their jurisdiction.

But then it was the prosecution's turn to act strangely. With such a clear confession to work with, quite why they needed to claim the following is uncertain. The attorney argued that Ross had given Malchik directions to a crime scene. Malchik said that, oddly, the directions had been lost from both the written and taped statements. For his part, Ross was happy to confess to the crimes, but not to giving these directions.

The trial was to be handled by Superior Court Judge Seymour Hendel, and he was furious that the prosecution and police seemed determined to lie to the court and mislead it. During a closed hearing, he let vent his anger and some of the charges against Ross were dropped.

But despite this, Hendel allowed the police to put forward their suspect account. The records of the closed hearing were subsequently sealed for two years, and when they were opened Hendel withdrew his attack on the authorities of law and order. The idea that this was not a trial enacted in a totally transparent way remained. In the end, Ross was convicted of killing four of the eight woman to whose murders he confessed. It took the jury just eighty six minutes to reach their verdict; of a more disturbing nature it took them then just four hours to decide upon the death penalty. One suspects a couple of more hard line, persuasive types were behind such a quick decision on a man's life.

But, in fact, the story was simply entering another phase. The question next to emerge centred around whether Ross was of sufficient mental acuity to understand the sentence given to him. Certainly, there were those who were completely confident that he was. One psychiatrist argued that Ross was a narcissist who experienced no genuine sympathy for his victims, or their families.

He was, claimed the apparent expert, a man completely without empathy. If indeed Ross was unable to feel any empathy, there are plenty who would make the case that such a condition was itself evidence of a severe and debilitating mental health condition. However, many felt that this was a man whose psychological problems were evidence that his crimes were the result of illness rather than evil. That he was a high performing sociopath, but one whose killing was the result of something beyond his control.

It may be that his childhood experiences had created this monster – the beatings, the denial of love from his mother, the sexual abuse he suffered at the hand of his young uncle. Perhaps even the trauma of a young child forced to kill chickens by strangling them with his small, bare hands. Equally, that madness could be genetic. Inherited from a mother who clearly and undoubtedly suffered from severe mental health problems. Possibly his adult behaviour was the consequence of both hereditary and learned factors.

During his close to twenty years on death row, Ross managed to fall in love with a woman. Susan Powers was from Oklahoma and although their engagement broke down in 2003, she continued to be close to Ross right up until his death. He also dedicated himself to learning braille and supporting his fellow inmates as they tried to come to terms with their own demons.

He became a devout Roman Catholic. That conversion would play a part in the final chapters of his story.

Initially, Ross opposed his death sentence. He accepted that he was guilty of the crimes and said that he deeply regretted his actions. Nobody had been executed in New England for more than forty years. In fact, he would be the last to die at the hands of the state before

Connecticut withdrew capital punishment from their sentencing options. It is strange, in these circumstances, that the exception should be made for Ross. One suspects political motivations.

However, suddenly in 2004, Ross appeared to become tired of the endless rounds of appeals and delays. The rapidity of his about turn was seen as evidence that this was a man who outwardly was a normal, intelligent being but who internally was as mixed up as it was possible to be. God had forgiven him, he claimed, and it was time to put the suffering of his victims' families to bed. He refused any further appeals, and asked for his execution to go ahead.

Cynics argued that his was just another attempt to get out of the sentence awaiting him. The very act of saying that he wanted to die could be used as evidence that he did not have the mental capacity to understand the sentence put upon him.

But unknown powers were at play, and despite the best efforts of his father, and his lawyer, it was decided that he was fit enough to die. He received a stay on January 26th, at the request of his father. Then, three days later his lawyer argued that he was suffering from death row syndrome, and was incapable of waiving his rights of appeal. It was all to no good. And so, on May 13th 2005, at 2.25 in the morning, Ross was executed by lethal injection at the Osborn Correctional Institution in Somers, Connecticut.

Later, Dr Stuart Grassian received a letter from the grave. It was written on 10th May, but not delivered until after the May 13th execution. Dr Grassian was the psychiatrist who argued that Ross was not in a fit condition to waive his appeals. 'Check and Mate,' read the note, which was from his patient. 'You never had a chance.'

Michael Bruce Ross committed atrocious crimes. His victims should never be forgotten, nor their suffering minimised as their deaths fade into the past for all but their families and friends. But he was a confused, psychopathic man. Alive, and with his willingness to help the authorities to learn about the conditions which led to his killing spree, he might have provided psychiatrists with information which would, in the future, prevent more victims. The evil brewing in some mentally ill citizens might have been addressed.

Dead, Ross offers nothing. Revenge was satisfied by his execution, the interests of victims to come were not.

MANSON'S BOY : BOBBY BEAUSOLEIL

JESSI GREEN

One of those Hollywood kids

Born on November 6, 1947 in Santa Barbara, California, Robert "Bobby" Kenneth Beausoleil didn't seem destined for stardom. He was the oldest child in a family of working class Catholics, with a father who put in twenty years as a milkman for Arden Farms before being promoted to a management position.

According to Beausoleil, there were no "severe problems" at home – he didn't suffer from any abuse and was a strong student in both the private and public schools he attended. However, he admitted that he was not close to his father, primarily because of his father's busy work schedule.

"He would work two jobs to support five children, and his family, and mortgage, and so on and so I didn't see him that much – I didn't really connect with him very closely," Beausoleil said during his parole hearing in October, 2016. "I started seeking outside of my home for identity, who I was, and I think it was partly just sort of adventurous spirit."

Even the two instances when he ran away from home, Beausoleil recalled, it wasn't out of anger or feeling neglected – it was "just wanting to see the world," he said. He even moved out of the bedroom he shared with two younger brothers and into "a little corner of the garage" when he was nine years old.

By the time he was twelve, Beausoleil was causing trouble. It started small, he said, "walking my dog without a leash, stolen Christmas tree ornaments, bomb scares, hitchhiking on the freeway" – but he found himself facing a year-long stay at the Las Priestas reform school when he was only fifteen. It was during his teenage years that the charismatic, good-looking Beausoleil earned himself the nickname "Cupid."

"I was one of those Hollywood kids," Beausoleil said, in a 1973 interview with Truman Capote. "I was in a couple of movies, but my folks were against it. They're real straight people. Anyway, I never cared about the acting part. I just wanted to write music and play it and sing."

Beausoleil remembers getting his first guitar at the age of eleven, finding it in his grandmother's attic and teaching himself how to play. Ever since, he said, he's been "nuts" about music – and packed up his guitar and headed south to Los Angeles to pursue his dreams when he was just sixteen years old.

"My grandma was a sweet woman, and her attic was my favorite place," he recalled. "I liked to lie up there and listen to the rain. Or hide up there when my dad came looking for me with his belt."

He started a band called Grass Roots, which would later be known as Love, before moving to San Francisco and playing with several different groups until the late 1960s. Many of Beausoleil's contemporaries have gone on to achieve successful careers in the music industry, including The Orkustra, which Beausoleil played with in San Francisco for two years.

It was there that Beausoleil met filmmaker Kenneth Anger, who wanted the charismatic and handsome young musician to play the lead role in his upcoming film, Lucifer Rising. Beausoleil agreed on the condition that he would collaborate with Anger to compose the film's soundtrack.

However, Beausoleil and Anger had a falling out, and he returned to Los Angeles for a role in a soft-core porn film called The Ramrodder – which was shot on the Spahn Ranch and co-starred Manson follower Catherine "Gyspy" Share. Cult leader Charles Manson found Beausoleil's musical abilities very impressive, and it wasn't long before Beausoleil became a follower himself. He spent a few months living with Manson's associate, Gary Hinman, before moving to the ranch with the rest of the Manson family collective.

"Everybody wants to know how I got together with Manson," Beausoleil said. "It was through our music. He plays some, too."

According to Beausoleil, he was out on the town with some of his "ladies" when they came across an old roadhouse with many cars parked outside. Upon entering the establishment, they found Manson with some of his "ladies," Beausoleil recalled, and all "got to talking."

"We played some together, and the next day, Charlie came to see me in my van, and we all, his people and my people, ended up camping out together," said Beausoleil. "Brothers and sisters. A family."

A member of the Family

In the beginning, Beausoleil said, he didn't see Manson as a leader, or an influencer. He had his people, Beausoleil contended, and "I had mine." In fact, he said, "if anybody was influenced, it was him. By me." Still, by 1969, Beausoleil had become one of Manson's chief recruiters – and later that summer, would participate in the torture and murder of his friend, Gary Hinman.

"Charlie made a commitment that he would be willing to die for his family," Beausoleil said. "And when you make this commitment, it's very easy to fall into the trap of 'I would be willing to *kill* for the family.'"

Hinman was a music teacher and a professional student who had befriended the Manson Family, allowing various members of the Family to live at his Topanga Canyon home whenever they needed a place to stay – including Beausoleil himself. According to Beausoleil, Hinman had given him "basic lessons" on how to notate, since he had never learned how to read or write music. But he said he wouldn't have considered Hinman a "close friend."

"Gary Hinman was not somebody you could be close with," said Beausoleil. "His ideologies were very different from mine. He was into communism and all that sort of thing – I couldn't relate to that at all. He was a political science major with a piano on the side for some kind of an income."

That July, Beausoleil went to Hinman's home with two other followers, Mary Brunner and Susan "Sadie" Atkins, who wanted to tag along because "they liked Gary Hinman." However, after holding the man hostage for two days, Beausoleil finally stabbed him – and used Hinman's own blood to draw the words "Political Piggy" on the wall.

"I'm not a nut. If I have to use violence, I'll use it, but I don't believe in killing," Beausoleil said. "I never meant to... to hurt Gary Hinman. But one thing happened. And another. And then it all came down."

Just another weird hippie

On July 31, 1969, a possible homicide at Hinman's address was reported to the authorities. Inside, police discovered Hinman's body along with the words Beausoleil had smeared on the wall. The body revealed stab wounds to the heart and a large slash across the left side of his face. Hinman's house had been ransacked, and his vehicles were missing. Still, with no leads, the police had resigned themselves to assuming the murder would go unsolved – just another weird hippie killed in Los Angeles.

But on August 5, 1969, Hinman's Fiat station wagon was spotted near San Luis Obispo by California Highway Patrol – with Beausoleil napping in the back seat. He had no driver's license, just a fake ID and a sheath knife holstered to his belt, and he claimed the car had broken down on his way to San Francisco. Shortly after he was found with the dead man's car, Beausoleil was booked for Hinman's murder.

"I was kind of devastated by what I had done," Beausoleil said. "I drove the car off on the pretense of ditching it somewhere. I picked up some hitchhikers and took them to where they were going and just continued north. In retrospect, it was definitely a stupid move."

However, he maintains that he took the car and left in an attempt to "create as much distance between myself and those people" as he could. He drove away with nothing but his guitar, twenty dollars, and the clothes on his back – and it became one of the biggest mistakes of his life.

Helter Skelter

Beausoleil was arrested just days before Manson declared "Helter Skelter" and Family members murdered the actress Sharon Tate and four other people, and next night, killed grocer Leno LaBianca and his wife, Rosemary. Beausoleil's slaughter of Hinman on Manson's orders would be the first killing tied to the Manson Family.

"The media, they called us a 'family,' and it was the only true thing they said," Beausoleil said. "We were a family. We were mother, father, brother, sister, daughter, son. If a member of our family was in jeopardy, we didn't abandon that person. And so for the love of a brother, a brother who was in jail on a murder rap, all those killings came down."

According to Beausoleil's interview with Truman Capote in 1973, it's possible that these infamous murders were actually committed in the hopes of freeing Beausoleil. Capote reasoned that by committing similar homicides, the Manson Family would prove Beausoleil's innocence – if he was incarcerated at the time of these follow-up killings, how could he be guilty of Hinman's murder?

"That is to say, it was out of devotion to Beausoleil that Tex Watson and those cutthroat young ladies, Susan Atkins, Patricia Krenwinkel, Leslie Van Houten, sailed forth on their satanic errands," Capote wrote.

Beausoleil has said that he thinks his murder of Hinman had a "triggering effect" on the Manson Family, spurring them on to commit more crimes. But he feels the "noble concept" of rescuing Beausoleil from prison provided many of the disciples with a "twisted and bizarre" justification for carrying out the Tate and LaBianca murders.

"You've got to understand that these people were not totally without some kind of scruples," Beausoleil said. "What the exact motives were, I can't really say ... I've seen it a lot in here, where people are so desperate that they really don't know who to strike out at. It was more that sort of thing than something that was sat down and plotted out."

Beausoleil has admitted since that he regrets the murder, for many reasons. In his most recent parole hearing, he said he should have taken Hinman to the hospital immediately after he was injured – and he would have, Beausoleil said, if he'd "truly been the man that I wanted to be, that I wanted to be then."

"The thing that I think I regret the most is not having the courage to do that, to face down the fear, and anxiety, and paranoia that I was kind of experiencing at that time," he said. "And to do the right thing by him."

Even as the situation began to escalate between Beausoleil and Hinman, Beausoleil claimed he was still trying to think of ways to resolve the dispute without anyone getting seriously injured or calling the police. When it finally dawned on him that Hinman had already sustained serious injuries and there would be no way to get out of the situation without involving the authorities, Beausoleil said his "fear" pushed him to take Hinman's life.

"It's so hard for me to say it, because it's so totally not what I would have wanted to do to anyone," he said. "I mean, after this happened, I was – I was a shattered individual."

Questionable motives

Theories have surfaced that Manson had asked Beausoleil to smear the words on the wall to make the murder look like a killing by the Black Panther group, in an attempt to start a race war. According to Manson prosecutor Vincent Bugliosi, who wrote a book about the Family, Hinman's murder was intended to be the start of "Helter Skelter," the "war" that would Manson preached would break out during the summer of 1969.

However, Beausoleil maintains that he wasn't "thinking about blacks, necessarily" when he had Susan Atkins write the words.

"Gary Hinman was into his revolutionary communism – his whole living room was a library of communist literature," Beausoleil said. "I figured I'd make it look like one of his cohorts, you know?"

Even after more than 40 years, the motive is still unclear. Conflicting reports have emerged, even from Beausoleil himself, around the reason for the brutal killing. One version of the story details how Manson sent Beausoleil and the two others to the house to collect money Hinman allegedly owed the family.

Another version is that Beausoleil had sold 1000 tabs of mescaline to Manson's friend, Danny DeCarlo, club treasurer for the *Straight Satans*, a local motorcycle gang. Just a few hours later, Beausoleil alleged, the bikers demanded their money back, claiming the tabs were actually strychnine. Since Hinman had purportedly manufactured the questionable drugs, Beausoleil had gone to collect the reimbursement – and things took a turn for the worse.

"I could have said, you know, I'm not a thief, Gary's my friend, Gary's a good man, he's done nothing to deserve any sort of mistreatment, having anything taken from him," Beausoleil said. "And stood up to these guys who were trying to convince me that he had sold them, through me, something that they didn't appreciate."

But Beausoleil felt intimidated, he said, by the bikers, and likely would have "taken a beating" if he'd refused to collect the refund.

"There had been some suggestion that I tortured him, a theory used by the district attorney to justify a first degree conviction, a felony murder," Beausoleil said.

Claims have also surfaced that Manson himself may have even been present at the time of Hinman's death – Beausoleil has claimed both that Manson was never there and that Manson first sliced Hinman's face with a "sword-like knife" before ordering Beausoleil and his other followers to finish him off.

During Beausoleil's most recent parole hearing, Presiding Commissioner Labahn specifically asked why Beausoleil murdered Gary Hinman.

"I'm not looking for a logical explanation for a crime which, I believe, based upon my preparation for today's hearing, defies logic," Labahn said. "I am interested in what you now recognize as causative factors that led to you murdering Mr. Hinman."

Beausoleil's response to the question appears heartfelt – he explained to the commissioner that although he wasn't necessarily interested in being a criminal himself, he felt a "desperate need" to prove himself, to impress contemporaries who were "somewhat criminally oriented."

"I really felt inadequate, you know, around some of these guys," he admitted. "But I wanted to – I wanted to find acceptance, I wanted to find a sense of belonging ... A lot of it was romaticization, I was romanticizing what kind of people they were. I was seeing my fantasy of what they were ... at that time, I wanted the acceptance of people that were in that circle."

According to Beausoleil, the music industry at that time, during the late 1960s, had started to "disintegrate." He struggled with feelings of distrust and resentment toward the industry as a whole, and had started gravitating more to what he said were "other areas."

"There was never a time, I don't think, not even now, when there was such a division in the country – and the level of violence that was emerging," Beausoleil said. "I did feel certain inadequacies in the world, in the fraternity of men."

Even then, however, Beausoleil claims he wouldn't have considered himself a "dangerous person." Rather, he was simply pursuing "wholesome needs," but using the wrong strategies to achieve the acceptance and belonging he so desired.

A much-anticipated trial

The case first went to trial in November, 1969, resulting in a hung jury. Beausoleil likely would have been acquitted of his crime, but *Straight Satans* motorcycle gang member Danny DeCarlo was brought in by the police on unrelated charges. In exchange for immunity from charges ranging from drug dealing to car theft to gun smuggling, DeCarlo provided the state with substantial evidence against Beausoleil.

In March, 1970, Beausoleil's case went to trial for the second time –
following extensive media coverage of Charles Manson and his Family
cult. This time, the prosecution sought the death penalty in addition to
a conviction for first degree murder. In his closing remarks, Beausoleil
reportedly quoted Bob Dylan.

"You can't judge me – there is no possible way to feel any remorse,"
he said bitterly. "Only God can judge me, and God is on my side."

More than a decade went by before Beausoleil would finally confess
to the crime. He continued to proclaim his innocence even from
behind bars, until an interview in 1980 where he told a reporter about
his guilt – and the Manson Family relationships and motives that led
to Hinman's murder.

However, he has opened up since about what led him to make the
angry statement he made to Judge John Shea at the end of his trial.

"As far as I'm concerned, that man is a hell of a lot more diabolical
than Charlie Manson ever was," Beausoleil said. "But the thing is, I've
felt a great deal of remorse within me. I think I wanted to pay for Gary
Hinman's death. I think I owed Gary that ... It was a big mistake. You
can't give a life back."

A prolific creative

Beausoleil's sentence was commuted to life in prison in 1972, after
the death penalty was ruled unconstitutional by the California
Supreme Court. In 1994, Beausoleil was relocated to a penitentiary in
Oregon at his request, after he married a woman from Oregon while in
prison – and later fathered four children. Beausoleil was moved back to
California in 2015, following the death of his wife and a disciplinary
infraction at the Oregon prison. He is currently held in California
Medical Facility in Vacaville.

During his time behind bars, Beausoleil is said to have joined the
Aryan Brotherhood, becoming what Capote referred to as their
"ringleader," although he denied this in a statement posted to Facebook
in 2014. He has also continued to create – even completing the

soundtrack to Anger's Lucifer Rising in the late 70s. Much of his music is played with instruments he's constructed himself, including a guitar-esque synthesizer that he's named the Syntar.

"I started making music with the guys in San Quentin – eventually, we put together a little talent show," said Beausoleil in a 2015 interview with VICE. "From that point, it was a gradual evolution or gradual navigation, I think is the better word to put it, to put myself into a position to be able to do music in earnest."

Beausoleil has even taught himself digital animation over the years. In 2014, he released the first segment of a cartoon called Professor Proponderus which he hopes will help kids with family members behind bars understand and come to terms with the situation. He has maintained a prolific presence online, using his website to sell the artworks and music he produced while stuck behind bars.

Oregon authorities had granted Beausoleil permission to record and sell his music, but state authorities in California denied his request. Still, Beausoleil has continued to make and release music, which has significantly impacted his chances for parole. According to some reports, the board has found that Beausoleil's continued musical and artistic endeavors are "exploitative" of his crime.

"If he can't play by the rules in place within prison, how can he play in a free society?" said Debra Tate, sister of Sharon Tate, who was murdered by the Manson Family while Beausoleil was in prison.

According to Beausoleil, though, "society doesn't respect its own laws." He continues to live by his own laws and his own "sense of justice," he said, with the belief that "what goes around comes around."

He has also said that he feels his artistic pursuits have helped in his efforts to rehabilitate – and that the kind of justice that involves sentencing prisoners to "a living Hell" behind bars doesn't make better citizens. Instead, he argues, it "turns them into monsters."

"There are people, perhaps well-intentioned, who are adamant in their stance that prison is for punishment, and that people who are doing time for a crime should not be permitted to engage in activities that do not strictly conform to this narrow definition," he wrote in a post shared on his own website in November, 2016.

Instead of becoming a "monster" like many other inmates forced to spend their days and nights in tiny cells, Beausoleil said he has rechanneled his "destructive or self-destructive tendencies" through "creative self-expression" – aligning himself with a more positive path to move forward. A path to redemption.

"Because I had deprived the world of what gifts Gary Hinman might have brought to it in the fullness of his life, I felt the need to redouble my efforts and to try to do more than I might have otherwise, in the hope that I might make up for that a little bit," he wrote. "In the end, I am not the one to say how successful I may have been in this mission I've been on these past 40-plus years. What I can claim with confidence is having given it a solid effort."

It's with this goal in mind that Beausoleil said he continues to create and publish his work – even though it continues to threaten his likelihood of ever being granted parole.

"There is absolutely no doubt in my mind, if released, Bobby will be just a model citizen," said his attorney, Jason Campbell. "I think he's a very insightful and introspective person, and there is nothing about him that is dangerous."

Living behind bars

He was denied parole for the 18th time in October 2016 – more than 47 years after being convicted of Hinman's murder. He will be eligible to reapply in 2019, when he will be 71 years old. According to a statement from Los Angeles County District Attorney Jackie Lacey, parole was denied to Beausoleil due to the "heinous nature of the murder," since Hinman was stabbed to death on the orders of Charles Manson. She added that the court felt that the 68-year-old Beausoleil "remains a danger to society."

Another ongoing concern raised by the board during the hearing is the questionable motive behind Hinman's murder – Beausoleil's dangerousness could be evaluated differently depending on whether the killing took place over a simple drug deal gone bad or in an attempt to create a nationwide race war.

"Thank god," said Hinman's cousin Kay Martley, following the announcement of the probation board's ruling. "He killed, murdered my cousin, and it was gruesome. Three days, they kept him and tortured him. All of this just comes back, even after 47 years."

California Governor Jerry Brown has strictly refused parole to many of the surviving Manson Family members. In January 2016, Brown reversed the decision of the parole board to allow the release of 74-year-old Bruce Davis, who was convicted of the murder of stuntman Donald "Shorty" Shea, at Manson's request. In July 2016, he denied parole to Leslie Van Houten, 67, currently serving a life sentence for the killings of the LaBiancas.

Even Manson himself, now 81, has been refused parole twelve times. While some reports claim the parole board may go easy on Beausoleil in 2019, since he was so young at the time of the murder and he is nearing the end of his life, there is a good chance Beausoleil will live out the rest of his years behind bars.

"I don't think I belong in prison," Beausoleil said to VICE in 2015. "I mean, I'm not a threat or a danger to anybody, so in that respect it doesn't make sense that I remain. But nor is it the nature of my success. So yeah, I would say yes, I have restored myself to integrity."

Still, Beausoleil hopes to one day get out of prison so he can interact with his many fans in a more "normal" way. Even back in 1973, when Truman Capote asked him what he would rather be doing instead of spending his days behind bars, Beausoleil had vivid dreams for his future.

"Tripping," Beausoleil told him. "Out on my Honda, chugging along the Coast road, the fast curves, the waves and the water, plenty of sun. Out of San Fran, headed Mendocino way, riding through the redwoods. I'd be making love. I'd be on the beach, by a bonfire, making love. I'd be making music and balling and sucking some great Acapulco weed and watching the sun go down."

THE HILLSIDE STRANGLERS

NAOMI ROBERTS

Cousins Kenneth Bianchi and Angelo Buono, Jr. are collectively known by their media epithet "The Hillside Strangler". These two men were responsible for the murders of at least nine females, ages 12 to 28, during the late 1970s in Los Angeles, California, and Bianchi killed two more in Washington. After their first three victims did not gain much attention because they were prostitutes, Bianchi and Buono decided to abduct and murder middle-class "nice" girls. Five victims were found on hillsides in the Glendale-Highland Park area during Thanksgiving weekend in 1977 and the resulting panic led to the coining of the moniker "Hillside Strangler".

Lead Los Angeles Police Department homicide investigator Detective Sergeant Bob Grogan, along with his partner Dudley Varney as well as Los Angeles Sheriff's Department's Detective Frank Salerno, believed that the murders were the work of more than one killer but figured the less the murderers knew about what police knew the better.

Bianchi later moved to Washington where he murdered two more women before being caught.

Both Bianchi and Buono were convicted of multiple counts of first-degree murder and sentenced to life. Buono dies of a heart attack on 21 September 2002 while serving his time in Calipatria State Prison in Calipatria, California. Bianchi continues to serve his sentence at Washington State Penitentiary in Walla Walla.

Early Lives

Kenneth Bianchi

Kenneth Alessio Bianchi was born on 22 May 1951 in Rochester, New York, to a 17-year-old alcoholic prostitute who gave him up for adoption two weeks after he was born. He was adopted by Nicholas Bianchi and Frances Sciolono and despite a stable upbringing, Bianchi became a pathological liar at a very early age. Further, as a result of petit mal seizures he suffered at the age of five, Bianchi often daydreamt as if he were in a trance.

Bianchi suffered from insomnia and frequently wet the bed as a child (one of the triad symptoms of serial killers). Frances took him to the doctor on multiple occasions for his urination problem and being examined by the doctor caused Bianchi much embarrassment and humiliation. He also had a bad temper and was diagnosed with passive-aggressive personality disorder which is characterized by an individual who may appear to be enthusiastic about and actively comply with others' desires and needs while simultaneously resisting them, thus resulting in increased anger and hostility. At the core of this disorder is that the sufferer resents responsibility and instead of openly expressing his or her feelings, demonstrates said resentment through actions such as procrastination, forgetfulness, and inefficiency. Despite having a rather high IQ of 116, Bianchi was a chronic underachiever in school. When Frances took him to a psychologist, it was determined that Bianchi was overly dependent upon his mother.

On 2 January 1957, Bianchi fell off of a jungle gym and landed on his face. His mother then sent him to a private Catholic elementary school where he excelled in creative writing. In July 1963, Bianchi pulled down a six-year-old girl's pants after "spontaneously decid[ing] that he liked doing so".

His adoptive father died in 1964, thus leaving an unemotional Bianchi having to attend public high school where he joined a motorcycle club and dated frequently. His adoptive mother was forced to work and she was known for keeping Bianchi home from school for extended periods of time.

While in high school, Bianchi set high standards for his many girlfriends such as complete fidelity and outwardly absolute devotion; however, these standard did not apply to him.

He graduated in 1971 from Gates-Chili High School in Rochester and, soon after, married his high school sweetheart, Brenda Beck; however, the couple divorced after only eight months. Rumor has it that Brenda left without a word.

Bianchi enrolled at Monroe Community College to study police science and psychology after deciding that he wanted to become a police officer; however, after only one term he dropped out and then was rejected for several positions both in Rochester and, later, Los Angeles. Consequently, Bianchi worked a series of menial odd jobs, eventually becoming a jewelry store security guard for which he was fired for stealing and giving his girlfriends the stolen jewelry. He would steal from other employers over the years.

He then left Rochester and moved to Los Angeles in late 1975 at the age of 26.

Angelo Buono, Jr.

Angelo Anthony Buono, Jr. was born on 5 October 1934, also in Rochester, New York, to first-generation Italian-American immigrants originally from San Buono, Italy. His parents divorced when he was young and a five-year-old Buono moved to Glendale, California, with his mother Jenny and his sister Cecilia, where his mother supported the family by doing piecework in a shoe factory. Raised Catholic, this had no effect on Buono's development as a decent human being.

Buono displayed a very high interest in sex from a young age and when he was a teenager claimed that he had raped and sodomized number of girls. Buono idealized serial rapist Caryl Chessman, also known as "The Red Light Bandit", calling Chessman his hero but added that Chessman should have murdered his victims. He developed a deep loathing of women and desire to injure and humiliate them, including his mother who he would verbally abuse; however, he was emotionally tied to her until her death in 1978.

Buono began stealing cars and was sent to the Paso Robles School for Boys.

In 1955, Buono married his high-school sweetheart, Geraldine Vinal, who was 17 years old at the time, who he had impregnated; however, less than a week later he left her. She would later give birth to a son, Michael Lee Buono, on 10 January 1956. Buono filed for divorce and refused to pay child support or let his son call him "Dad". He was back in jail for car theft when his first son was born.

Later, he impregnated Mary Castillo who gave birth to his second son, Angelo Anthony Buono III, at the end of 1956 and then married her in 1957. The couple would have four more children: Peter in 1957, Danny in 1958, Louis in 1960, and Grace in 1962. In 1964, Buono was believed to have sexually assaulted his two-year-old daughter Grace; however, there is insufficient literature to know fully the circumstances of the allegation. Buono's second marriage to Castillo also ended in divorce that same year after she purported that he had been physically, emotionally, and sexually abusive toward her. In a last-ditch effort to reconcile with him, Castillo was "rewarded" with his handcuffing her and threatening to kill her at gunpoint. Castillo would later recount a night during the first year they were together where Buono tied her spread-eagled to the bedposts and "raped her so violently she was afraid that he was going to kill her" and "her pain seemed to him his greatest pleasure" and, thus, he had no qualms of hurting her and didn't seem to care that the children witnessed the abuse. He avoided paying child support again.

Buono married a third time in 1965 to a 25-year-old single mother named Nannette Campino and the couple had two children of their own: Tony in 1967 and Sam in 1969. Despite being treated as poorly as Mary Castillo had been, Campino feared for her life on a daily basis but stayed until he began to sexually abuse her 14-year-old daughter. Buono allegedly bragged that he raped his stepdaughter because "[s]he needs breaking in" and then turned her over to his sons for their pleasure. Campino finally took her children, filed for divorce, and fled the state in 1971.

Buono, again, was arrested for auto theft and was sentenced to one year in prison; however, due to his large family his sentence was suspended so he could work to support them.

Buono married yet again, on a whim, to a woman named Deborah Taylor; however, the couple did not live together, nor did they ever divorce.

In 1975, he became a car upholsterer and purchased his own place at 703 E. Colorado Street to live and work. Despite his abuse, cockiness, overbearing nature, and lack of good looks, Buono was considered very attractive by women, particularly younger ones who were usually naïve about sex so it was easy to convince them that his outrageous demands and proclivities were normal. Thus, he frequently forced women to engage in sex acts with him and began a relationship with a teenage girl whom he twice impregnated.

He was ugly inside and out; very coarse, vulgar, ignorant, selfish, and sadistic.

Bianchi and Buono Together

At the age of 41, Buono came into contact with his cousin Kenneth Bianchi, the latter who, in 1975, moved to California and in with his cousin. Bianchi found his older cousin with "dyed black hair, gold chains around his neck, a large gaudy turquoise ring on his finger, red silk underwear and a virtual harem of jailbait girls". Buono taught Bianchi how to use fake police badges in order to coerce free sex from prostitutes. When they needed money the two also became pimps for a short time until the two girls who worked for them—Sabra Hannan and Becky Spears—escaped after enduring relentless abuse by Buono. Bianchi, still desiring to become a police officer, applied for jobs at the Los Angeles Sheriff's and Glendale Police Departments but neither were hiring. He then procured employment with a title company and used his first paycheck on an apartment and a Cadillac, moving in with coworker Kelli Boyd. Boyd rejected his marriage proposal as she considered Bianchi to be very jealous, immature, and a liar; however, in May 1977 she told him she was expecting their first child together. The couple moved to an apartment at 1950 Tamarind Avenue in Hollywood.

Bianchi also rented some office space and set himself up as a psychologist with a fake degree and credentials. He did not have many clients and when Boyd found out she was outraged. During the "Hillside Strangler" investigation, Bianchi told Boyd he had lung cancer and was undergoing chemotherapy and radiation to explain for his work absences; however, this was a lie. One day, detectives came to his apartment to ask questions but were "favorably impressed" and did not consider him a suspect at that time.

The Murders

In October 1977, the two men committed their first murder together. Their M.O. was to cruise around Los Angeles and use fake badges to convince women that they were undercover police officers. After persuading them into Buono's car that the men said was an unmarked police car, the two would take their victims to Buono's house where they would rape, torture, and strangle them with their "signature" weapon—a garrote (a handheld ligature such as a chain, rope, or strap)—although some of their victims were reportedly killed by lethal injection, electric shock, and gas asphyxiation. Their bodies were thus disposed of outside, frequently in hilly areas.

Yolanda Washington, 19

19-year-old tall, leggy, African-American prostitute Yolanda Washington disappeared on 17 October 1977 from Cathedral City, California. She was found the next day dumped just outside Forest Lawn Cemetery, beaten, raped, and strangled with a piece of cloth. Her corpse was cleaned and there were faint marks around her wrists, ankles, and neck. Her body was posed in a grotesque sexual position.

Judith Lynn Miller, 15

On 31 October, 15-year-old Judith Lynn Miller, a runaway, was found in a La Crescenta-Montrose neighborhood, face up on a parkway in a residential area. The homeowner covered her with a tarp so that neighborhood children wouldn't see her. After the incident, that same homeowner relocated his family to another state.

The victim was small and thin, perhaps 90 pounds, with medium length reddish-brown hair. She had bruising around her neck. She had also been raped and sodomized and her body had been posed with her legs in a diamond-like position.

Los Angeles Sheriff's Department Sergeant Frank Salerno was called to the site. He noticed insect activity upon her skin and on her eyelid was "a small piece of light-colored fluff" that he saved for forensic experts. He surmised that she had been killed elsewhere and her body had been deliberately placed where it would quickly be found.

At her autopsy, the coroner determined that she had been killed around midnight and was raped and sodomized.

There was no missing person's report matching this latest victim so after a couple of days, Salerno had the newspapers run a small story on her with a request to contact the police if anyone could identify her. Still nothing. Salerno then took her picture to Hollywood Boulevard and showed it to hundreds of runaways, addicts, homeless people, and prostitutes. The name Judy Miller kept coming up as a young destitute prostitute. One man named Markust Camden—a self-proclaimed bounty hunter—told Salerno that he saw Judy Miller leave the local fish and chips restaurant at 9:00 p.m. the night before she was found dead. In fact, he would pick Buono out of a police photo lineup, but failed to recognize Bianchi.

Eventually, Salerno was able to track down the Miller family and got a positive identification. They had nothing useful to contribute to the investigation.

Elissa "Lissa" Teresa Kastin, 21

Lissa Kastin, 21, was working as a waitress at the Healthfaire Restaurant to pay for ballet lessons as she was an avid dancer. She also worked part time for her father's real estate and construction business. She was last seen leaving work the night of 5 November. She was found the next day near the Chevy Chase Country Club in Glendale on 6

November; which was also near to where Buono lived. She had been beaten, raped, and strangled to death.

Salerno compared notes with the Glendale Police Department and noticed similarities between his latest victim and this new one. Both bodies had the same five-point ligature marks—ankles, wrists, and neck—and had been dumped within six miles of each other. This latest victim had been raped but there was no evidence of sodomy.

When Salerno looked at the dump site he was confident that at least two men were involved due to the large guardrail between the street and where the body was found and the near impossibility that one man could have gotten her body over it alone.

Dolores Cepeda, 12 and Sonja Johnson, 14

After their early murders failed to attract much publicity, Bianchi and Buono decided to find some younger victims.

12-year-old Dolores Cepeda and 14-year-old Sonja Johnson were abducted in Highland Park, California, on 13 November. They had last been seen getting off a school bus heading home from St. Ignatius School and approaching a large two-tone sedan that, reportedly, had two men inside.

Both young girls were found on 20 November in the hills between Glendale and Eagle Rock, near Dodger Stadium by a young nine-year-old boy who was treasure hunting in the trash on the hillside.

Los Angeles Police Department Homicide Detective Dudley Varney had been called to this site.

Kristina Weckler, 20

That same day, 20-year-old Kristina Weckler was found on the other side of the same hillside where Cepeda and Johnson were found.

Weckler was a quiet, loving, and serious honors student at the Pasadena Art Center of Design and lived in Glendale.

She was found nude, raped, tortured, and strangled to death as evidenced by ligature marks on her neck, as well as around her wrists and ankles. She had blood oozing from her rectum and bruises on her breasts. Weckler was the first victim to show additional overt signs of torture; having been injected with Windex glass cleaner she had oozing injection marks on her arms.

Los Angeles Police Department Homicide Detective Sergeant Bob Grogan—Varney's partner—was called to this site. He noticed that there was no indication of any disturbance of the foliage in the area or evidence that the body had been dragged there. Grogan made a mental note that she likely had been killed elsewhere and then carried and dumped in this location by one or maybe two men.

At this point, police were entertaining the idea that there was more than one killer and that they were becoming increasingly more sadistic.

Jane Evelyn King, 28

28-year-old actress Jane King disappeared in Los Angeles around 10 November 1977, and was found near the Los Feliz off ramp of the Golden State Freeway on 23 November. She had been sodomized and strangled and her body was badly decomposed. After King was found, Los Angeles Police Department officials—in addition to Glendale Police Department and Los Angeles County Sheriff's Department officers—created a task force to catch the "Hillside Strangler".

Lauren Rae Wagner, 18

18-year-old student Lauren Wagner lived with her parents in the San Fernando Valley. Her parents had gone to bed on 28 November, expecting their daughter to return home before midnight. The next morning, they found her car parked across the street with the door ajar.

Wagner was found later that day in a wooded area near Glendale's Mount Washington area. She was lying partially in the street, nude, with ligature marks on her ankles, wrists, and neck. Wagner, too, had been tortured as the palms of her hands contained several burn marks.

At the dump site was also a "shiny track of some sticky liquid, which had attracted a convoy of ants". Police considered that if the substance was saliva or semen from the killer then, perhaps, his blood type could be determined, as tests on semen found inside the earlier victims revealed nothing. It was later found that Bianchi was not a secretor, in that his blood type could not be determined by other bodily fluids. DNA testing had not come into popularity at this time.

When Wagner's father questioned the neighbors, it turned out that the woman who lived in the house where his daughter's car was parked, Beulah Stofer, saw Wagner's abduction. Stofer said that Wagner had pulled over to the curb at around 9:00 p.m. and two men had parked their car beside hers. After some type of disagreement, Wagner "ended up in the car with the two men".

When Grogan went to talk to the neighbor, she told him that she had just had a phone call from a man with a New York accent who told her to "keep her mouth shut about what she had witnessed or he would kill her". Stofer also told Grogan that the car was a large dark sedan with a white top and that one of the men dragged Wagner from her car into his while Wagner protested, "You won't get away with this!" Stofer described one man as tall and young with acne scars while the other was older and shorter, Latin-looking, and with bushy hair. She said she was positive that she would identify them again. This statement rang true when she picked both Bianchi and Buono out of a photo lineup shown to her by Grogan.

Kimberly Diane Martin, 17

Tall, blonde prostitute Kimberly Martin, 17, disappeared from Echo Park, California, and was found strangled to death on 13 December 1977 on a steep hillside on Alvarado Street. Martin had worked for the Climax "modeling agency".

Police believed they had two reasonably good leads in this case. First, Martin's last "client" called her to 1950 Tamarind, apartment 114; however, this turned out to be a vacant apartment. Secondly, the murderer called from a payphone in the lobby of the Hollywood Public Library on Ivar Street. Unfortunately, nothing came from these leads.

Cindy Lee Hudspeth, 20

On 16 February 1978, 20-year-old Bible school teacher and secretary at an Echo Park church Cindy Hudspeth was found in the trunk of her bright orange 1977 Datsun B210 that had been pushed over a cliff on Angeles Crest in Los Angeles National Forest near La Canada. She had been raped and strangled, with the strangulation marks similar to those associated with the "Hillside Strangler".

Hudspeth was also a neighbor of Weckler even though the two women did not know each other. Interestingly, Bianchi also lived in the same apartment complex; however, this lead was never pursued even though both Grogan and Salerno believed that there was a good chance that at least one of the murderers lived in the Glendale area.

After this case, the lack of additional victims resulted in the disbanding of the "Hillside Strangler" Task Force.

Jill Barcomb, 18 (originally believed to be a Hillside Strangler victim)

18-year-old prostitute Jill Barcomb was abducted in Beverly Hills and found near the famous Hollywood sign on 9 November. Whereas it was originally believed that she was a victim of the "Hillside Strangler" because she had been raped, beaten, and strangled, in 2005, her death was conclusively proven through DNA analysis to have been committed by Rodney Alcala, the "Dating Game Killer".

Also, sometime in 1977, the two men gave Catharine Lorre a ride with the intent of killing her; however, when they learned that she was the daughter of famous actor Peter Lorre who played a child murderer in Fritz Lang's 1931 masterpiece film *M*, they let her go. She had no idea who the men were until they were arrested.

The two stopped killing after their ninth victim, Hudspeth (although at this time it was presumed they had ten victims with Barcomb), likely due to the birth of Bianchi's son and, as some surmise, that he had made some acquaintances within the Los Angeles Police Department who would take him on ride-alongs around the city, ironically, looking for the killers, and Bianchi could talk about nothing else while in police presence. On the night they had tried to abduct another victim, the two men got into a heated argument when Bianchi told his cousin that he had been questioned in the "Hillside Strangler" case. After Bianchi's confession about being questioned by police, Buono, furious, threatened to kill his cousin.

Bianchi's Washington Murders

Bianchi's girlfriend, Kelli Boyd gave birth to their son, Sean, in February 1978, and in March Boyd decided to return to her parents in Bellingham, Washington, as she was tired of both Los Angeles and Bianchi's lifestyle. After three months of pleading to be reunited, Boyd relented and Bianchi moved to Washington in May. Bianchi's role as boyfriend and father was relatively successful and he even took a job as a security guard, ultimately earning the trust of his supervisors. However, this way of life did little to alleviate Bianchi's murderous urges. Within six months he was actively looking for new victims.

On 11 January 1978, Bianchi lured two Western Washington University students—roommates Karen Mandic, 22, and Diane Wilder, 27—to a house he allegedly "guarded" under the pretense of housesitting. Once there, he raped, tortured, and murdered them.

On 12 January, police were informed that two female students were missing after Mandic's boss became worried that she didn't arrive at work that day. He did remember that she had told him she had accepted a housesitting job in a wealthy Bayside neighborhood from a security guard friend of hers. When former-priest-turned-Bellingham-Police-Chief Terry Mangan went to the girls' home he found a hungry cat, as well as the address of the home where they were to housesit. The name of one security guard kept coming up, as well as a record that Bianchi had used a company truck that same night, supposedly to take into the shop for repairs. This never happened. Mangan began to consider the fact that the women had met with foul play.

Police then went to the Bayside house and found a wet footprint. They also interviewed a neighbor who told them that a security guard asked her to check on the house except for the night the women disappeared because "there was special work being done to the alarm system and he didn't want her to be taken as an intruder".

After a press conference, a woman called police to report that a car had been abandoned near her home in a heavily-wooded area. In the car were the bodies of Mandic and Wilder. Both had bruising and had been strangled to death.

Mangan had the security guard picked up. He gave them no trouble. His name was Kenneth Bianchi.

There was ample forensic evidence in this case; most notably foreign pubic hairs on the girls and fibers from the house's carpet matching fibers on the dead girls' clothing and shoes. Additionally, when police searched Bianchi's home they found several items stolen from job sites where he worked.

Remembering back to the "Hillside Strangler" cases in Los Angeles—and knowing Bianchi had lived there—Mangan called the police departments in California who had worked on the task force. He spoke to Detective Frank Salerno to whom everything finally made sense. Detectives tirelessly worked to link Bianchi to the strangler cases and were confident that he was one of the murderers.

Investigation and Arrest

Bianchi was not as careful this time, having left significant clues, most notably his car with California license plates was seen and subsequently connected to the addresses of two Hillside Strangler victims. Without mastermind Buono, Bianchi didn't have the wherewithal to cover his tracks.

Bianchi was arrested the following day, on 12 January 1979.

Buono was arrested on 22 October 1979, after Bianchi told police about his cousin's complicity in the murders.

Trial and Conviction

Prior to his 1981 trial, Bianchi decided to plead not guilty by reason of insanity and claimed to have a separate personality named

"Steve Walker" who had committed the murders. After several interviews by experts specializing in multiple personality disorder and hypnosis, it was determined that he was faking. Immediately after Dr. Martin Orne mentioned to Bianchi that in genuine cases of multiple personality disorder there are typically at least three personalities, Bianchi created another alter ego named "Billy", shortly followed by two more. It was later determined that the name "Steven Walker" came from a student whose identity Bianchi had previously tried to steal to enable him to fraudulently practice psychology. Further, in Bianchi's apartment investigators found several psychology books which laid credence to Bianchi's ability to fake the disorder. He was eventually diagnosed with antisocial personality disorder with sexual sadism.

During trial, there was significant physical trace evidence against the two men; including fibers from Buono's upholstery from his home and workshop on two of the victims; an imprint of a fake police badge on his wallet; and hairs from rabbits he had raised on another victim.

Bianchi agreed to plead guilty and testify against his cousin in order to get leniency, albeit uncooperatively (evidence of his passive-aggressive personality disorder).

Judge Ronald M. George—who would later become California Supreme Court Chief Justice—said during Buono's sentencing hearing, "I would not have the slightest reluctance to impose the death penalty in this case were it within my power to do so. Ironically, although these two defendants utilized almost every form of legalized execution against their victims, the defendants have escaped any form of capital punishment." On an interesting side note, George's roommate at the time was author Darcy O'Brien who, four years after the trial, wrote a book about the case.

Both men were sentenced to life in prison.

While incarcerated, Buono married mother-of-three Christine Kizuka in 1986 while she was visiting her husband—and father of her children—who was in the cell next door to Buono at the Los Angeles

County Jail, serving 18 months for assault with a deadly weapon. She worked as a supervisor at the California State Employment Development Department.

Whereas the 64-year-old Bianchi continues to serve his life sentence at the Washington State Penitentiary in Walla Walla, Buono died of a heart attack on 21 September 2002 while serving life at Calipatria State Prison in Calipatria, California. Denied for parole on 18 August 2010, Bianchi will next be eligible for parole in 2025.

Aftermath

Bianchi is also a suspect in the "Alphabet Murders"—also known as the "Double Initial Murders"—which occurred in the early 1970s in his hometown of Rochester wherein three young girls were raped, strangled to death, and dumped in the wilderness. At the time he worked as an ice cream vendor situated near two of the murder sites. On 16 November 1971, ten-year-old Carmen Colon disappeared and was found two days later in Churchville, New York, 12 miles from where she was last seen. 11-year-old Wanda Walkowicz disappeared on 2 April 1973 and was found the next day in Webster, New York, off State Route 104, seven miles from Rochester. Finally, on 26 November 1973, Michelle Maenza, 11, disappeared and was found two days later in Macedon, New York, a mere 15 miles from Rochester. They were called the "Alphabet Murders" because not only did the young victims have the same initial for their first and last name but they were also found in cities which began with the same letter.

Whereas Bianchi has repeatedly tried to get his name cleared from these murders he remains a suspect because his vehicle was seen near two of the murder sites.

Another series of murders with similar circumstances occurred in California in the late 1970s and investigators have hypothesized that they are connected to the Rochester "Alphabet Murders". In 1977, Roxene Roggasch, Paula Parsons, and Carmen Colon (like one of the original "Alphabet Murder" victims) were found raped and dead.

Whereas Bianchi was tried for six murders, DNA exonerated him of the California "Alphabet Murders".

A 2008 movie entitled *The Alphabet Killer* was very loosely based upon the murders, and in 2010 a book written by Cheri Farnsworth called *Alphabet Killer: The True Story of the Double Initial Murders* was released.

In 1980, Bianchi started a relationship with a Veronica Lynn Compton, who was a defense witness during his trial. Compton, a cocaine addict who was fascinated by serial killers, was working as a scriptwriter in Hollywood. On one of her numerous visits with Bianchi while he was incarcerated, she gave him a copy of her screenplay entitled *The Mutilated Cutter*, about a female serial killer, and asked for this input. Compton grew increasingly fixated and allegedly fell in love with Bianchi. Later, she was convicted and incarcerated for attempting to strangle a cocktail waitress who she had lured to a hotel in a ploy to have the world—and authorities—believe that the real "Hillside Strangler" was still on the loose and that the wrong man was incarcerated. To make it look like an authentic "Hillside Strangler" murder, Bianchi manipulated and used Compton as a means to get out of prison by giving her semen of his smuggled out of the facility in a rubber glove to plant on the body. Despite that DNA forensics had not been utilized at that time, semen could still be analyzed to demonstrate the killer's blood type; however, Bianchi was not a secretor. The intended victim managed to get away and Compton was tried and convicted of first-degree attempted murder and sentenced to life. Compton was paroled from prison in 2003.

In 1992, Bianchi sued Catherine Yronwode for $8.5 million for putting an image of his face on a trading card. He claimed his face was his trademark. The case was dismissed with the judge saying that if Bianchi's face was, indeed, his trademark during the murders then he would not have tried to hide it from police.

In 2007, Buono's grandson, Christopher Buono, shot his grandmother—Mary Castillo who was married to Buono at one time—and then committed suicide. Christopher was unaware of his grandfather's true identity until 2005.

Bianchi and Buono are immortalized in film. The 1989 film *The Case of the Hillside Stranglers*—based on O'Brien's book—starred Dennis Farina as Buono and Billy Zane as Bianchi. In the 2004 film *The Hillside Strangler*, Buono was portrayed by actor Nicholas Turturro and Bianchi was portrayed by C. Thomas Howell.

The 2006 movie *Rampage: The Hillside Strangler Murders* starred Tomas Arana as Buono and Clifton Collins, Jr. as Bianchi.

In 2001 the Discovery Channel aired an episode of *The New Detectives* that revisited the murders.

Bianchi and Buono have also been mentioned several times on the television show *Criminal Minds* as an example of killer teams with psychopathic predatory sexual sadist personalities who murdered their victims together.

STOCKWELL STRANGLER : The True Story of Kenneth Erskine

47

NATALIE MARSHALL

Kenneth Erskine, known as "The Stockwell Strangler" due to the geographic proximities of his murders, was a deeply troubled young man who had demonstrated worrisome signs of violence and schizophrenia from a young age. He was a gerontophile in that he had an unnatural sexual attraction to the elderly. Gerontophilia, essentially, is the opposite of pedophilia. Erskine would break into elderly men's and women's London flats and strangle them while they were in bed; after which he would rape and/or sodomize most of them. To demonstrate his own warped sense of love for his victims he would cross their arms across their chest, close their eyes, and tuck them into bed. Also, perhaps to hide his shame, he would turn his victims' family photographs face down. There was much speculation among mental health professionals that Erskine also suffered from schizophrenia from a very young age.

He was eventually convicted of seven murders and one attempted murder and sentenced to life in prison in 1988 at the age of 25. However, in July 2009, following an appeal his murder convictions were reduced to manslaughter on the grounds of diminished capacity and he received a hospital order to serve his life sentences at Broadmoor Hospital. While he has the potential to be granted parole in 2028, the trial judge's original order was that Erskine should spend at least 40 years behind bars, thus making him at least 65 years of age before potential eligibility for release.

Early Life

Kenneth Erskine was born in Hammersmith, London in July 1963. His mother Margaret was British and his father Charles was from Antigua. He was one of four boys, had an average IQ when tested at eight years old, and was remembered by neighbors to be a "chubby, Bible reading soul"; however, he became increasingly violent and difficult to control. For example, as a child, Erskine had tried to hang his younger brother, John, twice.

Erskine was then sent to a series of schools for maladjusted and troubled children where he received his formal education. He frequently and violently attacked his teachers and classmates and was identified as inhabiting a fantasy world with murderous impulses. In his own private fantasy world he would take on the role of Lawrence of Arabia, attacking and tying up smaller and weaker children—a theme that would resurface when he targeted the weaker elderly during his murder spree. During a school-sponsored swimming outing he had attempted to drown several classmates by holding their heads under the water until teachers were forced to intervene. He set fires at school and once pushed a classmate off of a moving bus. On another occasion he stabbed a teacher in the hand with a pair of scissors. In another event, a psychiatric nurse who tried to examine Erskine was taken hostage by him as he held a pair of scissors to her throat. He strangled the classroom guinea pig. Whenever any female staff tried to be empathetic and show him any type of affection he would expose his genitals or rub up against them.

There was frequent talk that Erskine demonstrated clear signs and symptoms of schizophrenia as a teenager but nothing ever came out of it. He never had therapy or medication or any real psychiatric evaluation.

By the time Erskine was 16 years of age he had turned to drugs and particularly enjoyed inhalants. This latest display of misbehavior was too much for his mother who eventually kicked him out of the house, forcing him to survive on his own. When Erskine tried to give his younger brother marijuana she finally disowned him. He never saw any of his family members ever again and was forced to spend the next seven years of his life "drifting through the twilight world of London's homeless and rootless" living in squats and hostels in Brixton and Stockwell and getting involved with petty crime which primarily took the shape of failed burglaries on primarily the elderly.

Erskine's violent tendencies continued to worsen.

When he was 18 he stabbed a young male with whom he was having a homosexual relationship at the time. Erskine had burst into his boyfriend's bedroom and stabbed and slashed at his body while he lay in bed. Whereas this may have been the first attack of someone in bed it was a glaring omen of the terror he would wreak in six years.

Erskine was described my many who knew him as a persistent loner who drifted through life and due to no direction of any type of social support system started a life of crime. Erskine was also a Rastafarian due to his Caribbean heritage but was shunned by fellow Rastafarians due to his habit of theft.

An unsuccessful burglar, he was jailed on many occasions.

Among Erskine's favorite "drugs" were solvents—such as glue—which he would inhale. Among the most oft-cited short term effects of huffing glue are hallucinations, delusions, and hostility. Long-term effects include depression, irritability, memory impairment, diminished intelligence, and serious and sometimes irreversible brain damage. There continues to be speculation as to whether Erskine was born with his psychopathic tendencies (nature) or whether his upbringing and environmental stimuli were to blame for his problems (nurture). The consensus is that a combination of factors worked together to create Erskine's sick and murderous persona.

Erskine subsequently spent considerable time in Borstals—youth detention centers—due to being apprehended following his many failed burglaries. While in one for burglary in 1982 Erskine would paint and draw pictures of elderly people in bed with gags in their mouths, with daggers in them, or burned to death. Additional pieces of "artwork" included headless figures with blood spurting out from their necks, people holding human hearts in their hands, disemboweled people, screaming faces, and copious pools of blood. Again, this was a chilling omen of what was to come. In one documentary about Kenneth Erskine and his crimes, one of his cellmates at Borstal, named James, described how horrific Erskine's paintings were and how he would frequently smile and laugh while painting them. As Erskine's only "friend" James became his confidant as well. The two would play chess to pass the time and then there were Erskine's disturbing paintings. James stated in an interview that Erskine always spoke very quietly—rarely above a whisper—and was very weird.

Borstal doctors were concerned enough to the point of asking the authorities not to ever free Erskine because they were seriously worried that he might try to replicate his paintings; however, he was, in fact, released and four years later he would begin his killing spree.

The Crimes

At some point Erskine decided to act out his fantasies and began to murder. He is classified as a geographically-stable serial killer who confined his murders to a specific area. As Erskine had no vehicle and roamed around the Stockwell area frequently confining his murders to this area was likely due to simple necessity.

The Stockwell section of South London is a favored place for the elderly to retire. In the summer of 1986, however, a serial killer conducted a reign of terror throughout the community that resulted in seven known deaths—and possibly another four—attributable to The Stockwell Strangler.

Eileen Nancy Emms, 78

Emms was a 78-year-old retired schoolteacher who lived in an "unkempt basement flat" on West Hill Road in Wandsworth. She was sexually assaulted and strangled by Erskine on 6 April 1986.

Emms' body was found on 9 April 1987 by her home help who, upon knocking on her bedroom door and receiving no response one morning, let herself in to find Emms in bed with the covers pulled up to her chin, seemingly asleep. There were no obvious marks upon her body. Initially, the cause of death was attributed to natural causes. The doctor called to the scene estimated that she died approximately three days earlier and signed a death certificate that stated natural causes.

Once the victim's home help noticed that her small portable television was missing, the police were called.

During her autopsy, the medical examiner revealed that Emms had been strangled by bare hands. There was heavy bruising to her chest which strongly suggested that her assailant had kneeled atop her while strangling her. Further examination revealed that she had been sodomized as the assailant had left semen around her anus.

A short Afro-Caribbean head hair was found on her sheet.

Janet Crockett, 67

Janet Crockett was Erskine's first July 1987 victim. She was chairwoman of her local tenant's association. Her body was found on 9 June in her flat in the Overton Estate in Stockwell. She had been strangled but, unlike Erskine's first victim—and subsequent ones—she was not sexually assaulted.

Police were able to immediately conclude that she had been murdered as she had considerable bruising on her chest due to sustaining two broken ribs as a result of someone kneeling on her while she was strangled to death. Additionally, her nightgown had been ripped from her body and folded neatly and placed upon a bedside chair.

Police also noticed that framed family photographs on the bedroom mantel had been placed face down or turned around. This action would be repeated at several of his crime scenes and speculation abounds as to what Erskine's underlying motive for doing this was. Some psychological experts have surmised that his anger at his own parents' rejection without a healthy outlet for his emotions led to an insane jealousy of normal family ties. Another hypothesis was that he felt ashamed at his actions and didn't want any "witnesses."

Police were able to find a smudged thumbprint on a displaced planter and a palm print on the bathroom window.

Pathologist Dr. Iain West conducted Crockett's autopsy and compared it to Emms. He concluded that their methods of strangulation were similar. He stated that with weaker elderly victims unconsciousness would occur within 30 second and death after approximately three minutes. While Crockett's and Emms' murders were similar—and that they were both elderly—police had nothing else to link the two victims.

Frederick Prentice, 73

In the early hours of 27 June, 73-year-old retired engineer Frederick Prentice was asleep in his council-run elderly people's home on Cedars Road in Clapham when he was awakened by the sounds of someone entering his bedroom. He saw a young man enter and Prentice turned on his bedside lamp and ordered the intruder to leave. Erskine then pounced atop the old man, placed his index finger to his own mouth as a threat for Prentice to be quiet, and then sat upon his chest where he alternated squeezing his windpipe powerfully, then relaxing his grip, and repeated this multiple times. Prentice told police that his assailant had whispered only one word over and over: "Kill." Prentice was able to push the alarm button near his bed which caused his assailant to leave.

After talking to Prentice the police were fairly confident that all of the victims thus far were, in fact, linked. A shoeprint found at the scene would also serve to connect this attack with some of the other murders.

Prentice would later identify Erskine in a lineup.

Valentine Gleim, 84, and Zbigniew Stabrawa, 94

The next day Erskine murdered 84-year-old World War II veteran Valentine Gleim and 94-year-old Polish immigrant Zbigniew Stabrawa in their adjoining rooms at Somerville Hastings House, an old folks' home on Stockwell Park Crescent. Both men had been manually strangled and sodomized.

The intruder had been seen by alert night duty staff but had vanished before the police arrived. Point of entry was, again, determined to be an open window. Staff were also able to see Erskine fleeing the scene and estimated his height at approximately five-feet-eight-inches with a slim frame so at least now investigators had a clue about their suspect.

Of particular concern in these two cases was the discovery of a used flannel towel and electric shaver which suggested that the murderer had calmly washed up and shaved after killing two people.

Approximately one hour prior to the double homicide an elderly woman in a Stockwell old folks' home was attacked while she was in bed by a man grabbing her arm. She fought off her assailant so vehemently that he had to run off. Her description of Erskine matched Prentice's.

William Carmen, 82

Two weeks after his previous double homicide, Erskine struck again by strangling and sexually assaulting 82-year-old widower William Carmen on 8 July. This time he threw a monkey wrench at detectives by murdering on the other side of the Thames river, in Islington, North London. Carmen was discovered dead in his bed in his flat on the Marques Estate by his daughter. As was the case with Erskine's other victims, Carmen was in bed with the covers pulled up neatly to his chin and had been sodomized.

This time there was clear evidence of ransacking and theft as approximately £400 of Carmen's savings was missing. Family photos were also placed face down or turned around.

William Downes, 74

On 20 July the body of 74-year-old William Downes was found by his son in his Holles House on Overton Road flat in Brixton; the same location where Erskine's second victim, Crockett, lived. He was naked and in bed with the covers pulled up to his chin, his eyes closed, and his arms folded across his chest—classic Erskine signature. Downes' son had reminded him to keep his windows locked firmly at night a few days ago so as not to fall victim to the Strangler but he failed to heed these instructions and point of entry was, again, determined to be through an unlocked window.

Downes had been strangled and sexually assaulted like the majority of Erskine's other victims. There were semen stains on the sheets.

Investigators lifted a palm print from the kitchen wall and another from the garden gate which were eventually matched to the prints found at Crockett's home. Finding the owner of these prints, however, was not as easy as the process is today. In 1986, while fingerprints were on file on computer discs at Scotland Yard, palm prints were not. Investigators had a stack of four million files; however, by concentrating on London-based burglars and petty thieves, they were able to compile a more workable load. They were subsequently able to match the prints to those Erskine, a small-time crook with an extensive rap sheet for burglary.

Unfortunately, the police did not know where to find Erskine and while they were looking he struck again, killing his final victim.

Florence Tisdall, 80

80-year-old partially blind and deaf Florence Tisdall was found in her apartment at Ranelagh Gardens near Putney Bridge on 24 July. The caretaker of the apartments noticed her walker in the communal corridor and knew something was wrong as Tisdall was unable to get around without it. He found her strangled, sexually assaulted, and with broken ribs as a result of her killer sitting atop her chest. She had spent the previous day watching the televised wedding of the Duke and Duchess of York—Prince Andrew and Sarah Ferguson—even having her own hair done especially for the big event. Tisdall had lived in an almost empty block of flats where she had resided for the past 60 years. A cat lady, she had left her windows open so the cats could come and go as they pleased and this is how Erskine got into her flat.

It was at this scene where Erskine made, perhaps, his biggest mistake. Detectives knew immediately that Tisdall had been murdered because she was found in her nightgown, tucked into bed with the covers up by her chin. In reality, however, Tisdall's neighbors who frequently checked on her because of her disabilities stated that she always slept atop the covers in the clothing she had been wearing that day. When Erskine undressed Tisdall to rape her, he attempted to cover up his misdeeds by making it look as though she went to bed as usual and died of natural causes. Family photos were also placed face down or turned around as was the case at the Crockett crime scene.

One of Tisdall's neighbors stated that she saw Erskine near the victim's flat shortly after the murder had occurred "looking disgusted with himself." Thinking this to be odd she promptly notified the police.

All of Erskine's victims were pensioners and in all but one case there was evidence of sexual assault that took the form of sodomy; however, investigators and forensic specialists cannot say whether it occurred before or after the victims' death.

Investigation and Arrest

After the Crockett murder, Scotland Yard's Serious Crimes Squad Detective Chief Superintendent Ken Thompson—a Scotsman with 26 years' experience—was put in charge of the case and given over 200 detectives to devote to the search for The Stockwell Strangler. Interestingly, Erskine was originally nicknamed "The Heatwave Killer" because the murders occurred during the summer; however, when the majority of his murders occurred in and around Stockwell this nickname was changed. Further, plainclothes officers would stand guard throughout the night wherever the elderly lived.

At the height of the investigation, as many as 350 law enforcement officers were on the Strangler case which included 150 detectives and senior officers from the C1 Murder Squad who worked out of five separate incident rooms throughout London which were linked to a special Home Office computer. This network was called HOLMUS and was used to prevent wasting time by cross checking paperwork which proved to be detrimental to the investigation for Peter Sutcliff, The Yorkshire Ripper. Other police officers set up fixed observation points in neighborhoods with a high population of elderly residents and instituted extra patrols.

A psychologist was enlisted to create a profile of the Strangler and to provide potential insight into his signature to determine whether he was attempting to cover his tracks or was fulfilling some bizarre fantasy. The suspect was determined to be suffering from gerontophilia; or a sexual attraction to the elderly and the complete opposite of its better known opposite, pedophilia. Speculation abounded as to whether the killer's sexual paraphilia was a result of some relationship problems with his grandparents. Additionally, as his victims were all selected at random, authorities could not link the victims together with the hopes of finding some commonality between them that would enable them to identify and apprehend the man responsible.

The suspect was classified as a process-focused serial killer. The majority of serial killers are of this type; the other being act-focused wherein their own psychological gratification from the kill itself is the underlying cause. Instead, process-focused killers achieve a hedonistic psychological "reward." These types frequently "get off" on the method of their kill and they enjoy the perverse sexual thrill that accompanies the act of killing. The literature identifies four types of process-focused serial killers: gain in which the killer kills for profit or personal gain; thrill in which the act of killing gives the killer a rush or a high; power in which the killer enjoys dominating and manipulating victims and while sex is usually involved it is primarily tertiary to the kill itself; and lust wherein murder is associated with sexual pleasure and this type of killer will commonly have sex while in the process or killing or may engage in necrophilia after death. As far as Erskine is concerned, he can be classified in multiple subtypes. First, since he did rob his victims and steal money he demonstrates some elements of the gain process-focused serial killer. Secondly, he did obtain a rush or high from killing his victims and, therefore, does demonstrate some elements of a thrill killer. This element is particularly salient when he was seen by a witness—who would later testify against him—getting sick on the sidewalk after his final kill near where his last victim was found. The act of his getting sick appears to be directly attributed to the thrill her received from killing and having sex with his victim. Finally, since Erskine likely sodomized his victims after he killed them his sexual fantasies were of a higher priority than is typically the case for power killers. Thus, he demonstrates elements more aligned with a lust killer.

Coupled with the fact that Erskine targeted the same type of people and that he engaged in specific rituals which were part of his signature makes Erskine a classic serial killer. His smaller size likely contributed to his choice of the elderly as his victims because in their weakened conditions he wouldn't have much trouble overpowering them.

The palm prints were the most damning evidence investigators had at that point; however, they only placed Erskine at two of the murder scenes. Despite similarities among all of the victims' crime scenes, the fact that Erskine wasn't cooperating with police required detectives to find other evidence. Investigators from Scotland Yard took the unusual step of distributing his Erskine's picture to the media to try to find more witnesses and potential leads by hopefully jog people's memories as to whether anyone may remember seeing him. Thompson also did something very uncommon; he appeared on television, appealing to Erskine to turn himself in.

After Tisdall's death the search for Erskine intensified even more than was already the case; however, being that he was a drifter with no permanent address or any real belongings to speak of they had to search through the hundreds of hostels and squats in South London. His life was so devoid of meaning and friends to help detectives find him.

Investigators got their big break when they realized that since the suspect was likely unemployed that he would be receiving social security and unemployment benefits. Upon further investigation they discovered that Erskine picked up his benefits on alternating Mondays from a Department of Health and Social Security office in Southwark, South London, and that he was due to collect his next check on 28 July. The building was placed under surveillance and when Erskine turned up, right on time, he was arrested and handcuffed without any struggle.

Whereas items and cash from the victims' homes were, in fact, missing, police did not believe that robbery was the driving motive in the homicides. There were neither signs of struggle nor any signs of forced entry. Police surmised that Erskine entered the flats through unsecured windows.

Forensic evidence linking the cases relied upon the fact that the victims were all murdered in similar ways: by the assailant kneeling on the victims' chests and then placing his left hand over their mouths and strangling them with his right hand. The semen collected at nearly all crime scenes suggested the same genetic fingerprint in that the same suspect was responsible for all of the sexual assaults. Additionally, there was a single hair found in Emms' flat, as well as matching shoeprints from three of the scenes.

A hairdresser informed investigators that Erskine had approached her wanting his head and pubic hair bleached. While she agreed to the former she refused the latter. Apparently, while he was sitting in the shop waiting for the bleach to take effect he self-applied the bleach to his pubic region and eyebrows, the latter resulting in his getting chemicals in his eyes and requiring assistance in washing it out.

When questioned by Detective Inspector Brian Jackson and other detectives, Erskine's responses indicated that the detectives' jobs were to be much more difficult than they thought. Erskine spent the majority of the interrogation giggling, staring out of the window or into the sky, or masturbating. After he was arrested, psychologists placed Erskine's mental age at 11 even though he was 24 at the time. He had first denied that he was, indeed, The Stockwell Strangler claiming instead to be a petty burglar who had no motive to kill anyone. After vehemently denying his culpability and blameworthiness in the string of murders and seeing that he wasn't getting anywhere, Erskine then changed his tune and said, "I don't remember killing anyone. I could have done it without knowing it. I am not sure if I did it." He also tried to blame the murders on a whispering female voice in his head. He once stated, "It tries to think for me. It says it will kill me if it gets me," and, "It blanks things from my mind."

He was clearly disturbed but not a fool in any sense. In fact, when searched, detectives found ten bank and building society accounts that Erskine had opened to hide the proceeds of his crimes. During the three-month span of murders, he had deposited over £3,000; quite a large sum of money for someone who was unemployed. This included a £350 deposit into one of his accounts on the morning after the Carmen murder. It was evident at this point that Erskine was amassing profits from his burglaries while simultaneously collecting unemployment benefits. This demonstrated that whereas Erskine did suffer from some degree of mental retardation and likely some psychosexual paraphilia he was not stupid by any means. In fact, he told detectives that his motive was to achieve notoriety. He said, "I wanted to be famous ... I thought I would never get caught."

During a lineup—or identity parade as it is called in England—surviving victim Frederick Prentice was able to definitively identify Erskine. Another woman who had witnessed Erskine vomiting on the sidewalk near Putney Bridge a mere 200 yards from the scene of the final murder on the night in question also picked Erskine out of a lineup.

Trial and Conviction

Erskine's trial commenced at the Old Bailey on 12 January 1988. He pled not guilty to the charges of seven murders and the attempted murder of Prentice. During his trial he would stare out the window or down at his feet as was the case when he was interrogated. When details of the murders were brought up, Erskine would masturbate.

The jury heard him confess to the burglaries of the deceased victims; however, he claimed that someone else must have followed him and killed the individuals after he had left. Nobody was buying this story.

After an 18-day trial, the jury unanimously found him guilty on all eight counts and he was sentenced to seven life terms plus 12 years for attempted murder with a recommended minimum of 40 years; one of the heaviest penalties ever handed out in British legal history. However, diagnosis of schizophrenia and other mental illnesses pursuant to the Mental Health Act of 1983 led to a successful appeal of Erskine's murder charges which were eventually reduced to manslaughter. He is currently serving his time at the Broadmoor Hospital.

In addition to his seven known victims, the police suspected Erskine of four other murders for which he has never been charged due to insufficient evidence to prove that he was, in fact, the murderer.

John Jordan, 57

On 4 February 1986, 57-year-old John Jordan was found in his Josephine Avenue flat in Brixton strangled beside his bed.

Charles Quarrell, 73

73-year-old Charles Quarrell was found suffocated in his bed on King James Street in Suffolk on 6 May. He had two handkerchiefs stuffed into the back of his throat, effectively blocking his windpipe.

Wilfred Parkes, 70

70-year-old Wilfred Parkes was found on 28 May in his Stockwell flat, suffocated and in bed. A nearby pillow was presumed to have been the murder weapon.

Trevor Thomas, 75

On 12 July 75-year-old Trevor Thomas was found dead in the bath at his home on Barton Court, Clapham. As Thomas had been dead for quite a while there was inadequate forensic evidence for investigators to link his murder to the others; thus resulting in Erskine not being charged with his death even though Thomas was almost certainly one of his victims.

As mentioned, Erskine has never been charged with these additional deaths; however, police were so confident that Erskine murdered them that they effectively closed the book on all of these cases. There is also much speculation that he likely killed prior to his first known victim—such as was the case with Mr. Jordan—and that because of his choice of victims their deaths may have simply been attributed to natural causes.

Aftermath

There is not much more information on Erskine due to a lack of any detailed studies of him as is commonly the case with other serial killers where the literature is rife with speculation as to what influences led to the individual turning to serial murder. His only possessions were meager clothes and some books from the building society. Other than a post-arrest diagnosis of schizophrenia, the mind of Kenneth Erskine remains mostly shrouded in mystery. In fact, his mentally-disturbed state has worsened to the point where he has been told that he will never be released from Broadmoor Hospital.

Psychiatrists have never been able to fully penetrate his mind and discover what makes him tick. He clearly has a problem differentiating fantasy from reality and appears to be locked in his own childlike world. However, there is one incident that clearly demonstrates his understanding between right and wrong. On 23 February 1996, Erskine prevented the possible murder of Peter Sutcliffe, known as the "Yorkshire Ripper" by alerting guards while another inmate, Paul Wilson, attempted to strangle Sutcliffe with the flexible cord from a pair of stereo headphones. Erskine was able to restrain Wilson from inflicting further injury upon Sutcliffe until guards arrived.

Erskine found himself on the receiving end of an assault. On Christmas Eve in 1997 he was attacked by fellow inmate, 34-year-old

Keith Hanger. Hanger was serving time for the 1992 shooting of his friend after having escaped from prison. He walked up to Erskine and squirted liquid from an aerosol can into his face before lighting it with a lighter. Erskine was taken to Frimley Park Hospital in Surrey, in agonizing pain and worried that he would lose his eyesight; however, his temporary blindness was just that—temporary.

Psychiatrists continue to attempt to probe Erskine's mind trying to uncover more and more of his psyche toward, perhaps, finding what makes him tick. Currently, he is unable to answer for his crimes, as demonstrated by the reduced sentence due to diminished capacity.titutes during the interrogation, which would explain why his DNA was found on three of the young girls' bodies. He focused on Tania Nichols, telling a story about how he picked her up with the intention to have sexual relations, but changed his mind and returned her back to the red light district. Again, this account differed from the one that he originally gave to investigators. On February 21, 2008, Steve Wright was charged as guilty on all five counts of murder after eight hours of deliberation. He received a life sentence without any chance of parole. On February 22, 2008, Wright was taken to prison, where he'll be forced to live out the rest of his years behind bars.

Wright is still alive to this day and he is having a terrible time in prison. His twisted state of mind after imprisonment is outlined in his letter to his father: "...I just wish everyone would get along and work towards a family unit because all the bickering and point scoring against each other is really getting me down it seems you are pulling me one way and pam is pulling me the other and in the end, something will give and it just seems to me that person will be me and that is the last thing that I want at the moment has I am sure you do as well because if I start to fall apart at the seams I don't think I could cope in here I need to be strong to cope with this nightmare like that but you said in the paper that when you looked [in] my eyes you would know whether I was guilty or not that really hurt me it was like a knife in the heart for you to even contemplate that I could even be capable of such a terrible crime. You say you want to help me the only way that will happen is if you make the effort to work together because all this he said she said you must understand is not doing my frame of mind any good I just want it to stop I do love you dad..."

The Racist Serial Killer

Nancy Meghan White

In Kansas City, Missouri, on August 18, 2017, Fredrick Demond Scott, age 22, was arrested and charged with two counts of first-degree murder and two counts of armed criminal action in the shooting deaths of John Palmer, aged 54, and Steven Gibbons, aged 57— the first and the last victims of the Indian Creek Murders. The Indian Creek Murders consisted of five white, middle-aged men. All were shot from behind and all except the last were shot on the walking and biking trails known as The Indian Creek Trail, thus the name Indian Creek Murders. Although Scott was arrested and charged on August 18, 2017, Jackson County Prosecutor Jean Peters Baker did not officially announce his arrest until August 27, 2017, when it was also announced that Scott was the suspect in the other three murders along the Indian Creek Trail.

These five murders happened over a span of nine months from August 2016 until April 2017 in a killing spree that left Kansas City men afraid to walk along trails alone and took police a year to solve only two of them.

After his arrest, Scott told investigators first that the gun fired accidentally as he pulled it from his pocket. Then police gathered DNA evidence that linked Scott to both the Gibbons and the Palmer murder scene. Scott then admitted to killing both men. Later, in an interview with investigators, Scott mumbled, "they [the victims] never saw it coming."

Scott told police that he was upset over the 2015 shooting death of his half brother, Gerrod Woods, with whom he had a very close relationship.

Gerrod was Scott's half brother by their father Tyrone Scott. However, his mother La'Kesha and her husband, Gerald Woods, Sr who adopted Gerrod, giving him the Woods last name, raised Gerrod.

Fredrick Scott was raised by his mother and has four living siblings, all of whom wish to remain anonymous. Scott's mother has said that Scott began exhibiting symptoms of paranoid schizophrenia at about the age of 16, as did his older brother. Scott, however, refused to get treatment for his condition and it worsened over the years.

On April 7, 2013, Scott's mother called police on him during an argument and in 2014, Scott was in court for assaulting his mother. Scott's mother says she was trying to get him to seek professional help at a mental health clinic for the paranoid schizophrenia. Scott was an adult and she could not force him to go. She did tell him on two occasions that he would have to move out if he did not "get himself together and get help." An argument erupted and Scott shoved her several times. This assault resulted in her calling the police. In January of 2014, while attending his senior year at Center Alternative School in Kansas City, Missouri, Scott found himself in trouble for saying that he wanted to "shoot the school up Columbine-style" and "kill the white people." Scott's mother said he never had any hatred toward white people that she knew about and that he even did odd jobs for a few white men. He received a suspended 180-day sentence for the threat against the Center Alternative School. Public records show that Scott was picked up for shoplifting in 2016.

Despite his troubles, Scott finished his term at Center Alternative School and graduated and received his diploma at the age of 20 after repeating his senior year. "His teachers and his principal were very supportive of him," Scott's mother said. "They really worked with him over there."

Scott worked odd jobs and had a job at a local Burger King in the vicinity of the murders. It is still unclear whether the killings were racially motivated, and some people are asking if one racist statement in the past can make these killings "hate crimes" or not.

People who know Scott said his half brother's murder sent him over the edge.

"He felt like his brother was the only person in the world who loved him," one of his Burger King co-workers told the Star. "It really damaged him."

In December of 2015, Scott's half brother Gerrod Hassan Woods, aged 23, was shot and killed along with another man during a robbery. This is the incident he cited as having him upset when he was arrested for the Gibbons murder. However, a black man killed his half brother, while Scott's victims were white, middle-aged men, most of them walking alone with their dogs. Gibbons was the exception. Video surveillance shows Scott follow Gibbons off a city bus. He then shot Gibbons and proceeded to turn around and get back on another bus. Therefore, Gibbons was shot on a city street whereas the other men were shot on the Indian Creek Trail or very near it.

Later, it was discovered that Scott had reported handguns as being stolen on four separate occasions. When asked if four separate stolen gun reports would not raise some red flags, Kansas City Police Captain, Stacey Graves said the department could not discuss the case against Fredrick Scott because the investigation is ongoing and still open, but she agrees that the stolen gun reports should have "raised some red flags." According to court documents that outline all five killings, the first three happened within days, and even hours, of Scott's stolen gun reports. Concerning the stolen gun reports, Graves also said, "That is something that is being investigated. It will be something we look at." It is still unclear when the fourth gun was reported stolen.

Of all the guns used in the killings, police have recovered only the 9 mm handgun, which, according to court records, Scott told detectives he used to kill Gibbons.

Scott had reported that gun stolen, also. Even though he denied any involvement in three of the killings, Scott told investigators he reported the guns stolen to disassociate himself from the killings.

Mark Jones of Chicago, a retired supervisory special agent in the ATF, said police should follow up immediately when someone reports a second gun theft because the victim is either complicit in the theft or the victim needs to better secure and protect firearms from theft. "I can see where you can report a gun stolen because you know it is going to be used in a crime, but I think you can only get away with that once," Jones said.

Kansas City Police Chief, Rick Smith, said at least 50 law enforcement personnel have worked on the investigation of the killings. The FBI assisted. On Tuesday, Smith said he extended his condolences to the families of the victims.

Police suspect that Fredrick Scott used the guns he reported stolen to commit these crimes and then reported them stolen to throw off investigators.

Brian Darby told The Star that he feels disrespected by the account given by Scott's mother that he suffers from paranoid schizophrenia. He feels the schizophrenia will be used as a defense for Scott.

THE INDIAN CREEK MURDERS:

Five middle-aged white men fatally shot from behind in sneak attack murders in Kansas City, Missouri. All victims were between ages 54 and 67, male, white, all but one were walking their dogs along Indian Creek Trail and in at least two cases, the dogs stayed by their slain owners until police arrived. The profiles of the victims made them relatively rare among Kansas City homicide victims. Some of the men were killed while walking their dogs.

The unsolved killings mystified Kansas City residents and spread fears of a serial killer.

First victim: John Palmer, aged 54, was shot several times, including in the back and his body dragged off the trail into the woods. He was found August 19, 2016 off East Bannister Road and Lydia Avenue in the small wooded area near the Indian Creek Trail. Police found a t-shirt at the scene with DNA that matched Fredrick Scott—who, a year later, under arrest for the Gibbons killing, admitted killing Palmer. Palmer was a man, who relatives said, liked to go on long walks through nature. Palmer's first cousin, Janelle Kristian of Olathe county, said he was, "a man of integrity, honesty and caring."

They grew up in the same household as children according to KANSASCITY.COM.

Second victim: David Lenox, aged 67,was found dead of a gunshot to the back of his head, only a few feet from his front door where he was walking one of his dogs, in the 9900 block of Walnut Street on February 27, 2017. A single .380-caliber shell casing lay close by the body. The police report that Lenox's dog stayed by his body until they arrived.

Third victim: Timothy S. Rice of Excelsior Springs, aged 57, was found dead on April 4, 2017, inside a shelter at Minor Park near East Red Bridge Road and 110th Street. He had been shot multiple times, including in the head. Police found several 9mm shell casings at the scene. Two hours after Rice was found, Scott reported a 9mm handgun stolen.

Hannah Rice, daughter of third victim, Timothy Rice, opened up about her dad and said she wanted the public to know him. "My dad was one of the friendliest people you could ever meet, he didn't know a single stranger," Hannah Rice wrote about her father in an email to The Star Monday evening.

She said in her message that her dad, who had been an electrician most of his life, "could make conversation with anyone at anytime." And, she said that after 13 years of being divorced, her dad and mom had remained friends and had lunch together on the day he died.

"I will always remember how he loved taking me as a child on hikes and fishing trips, we always would compete on who could catch the most fish. My father wasn't perfect by any means but he had a genuine heart," Hannah Rice wrote.

"No one ever expects something like this to happen in your life. To have your loved one brutally taken away from you," she said, adding that her heart goes out to the other four families who also lost loved ones.

Her message thanked Kansas City police for all their hard work on the murders. "They have done a phenomenal job chasing leads and working nonstop to catch this violent person," she said.

Hannah Rice also called for the public to provide police with help in the case.

"I also want to urge anyone to come forth with any information you may have no matter how small," she wrote. "It may just be the right information KCPD needs to see all of our families the justice we deserve."

Fourth victim: Michael Darby, aged 61, was found dead on May 18, 2017 from a single gunshot to the back of the head, along Indian Creek Trail off 103rd Street, about a half-mile east of the popular Coach's Bar & Grill where he was a co-owner. The bar was closed by flooding a month ago and may never reopen. The police found a single .22-caliber shell casing near the crime scene. The victim's son, Brian Darby, wonders if more could have been done to prevent the last deaths, including that of his father.

In June 2017, police released a 29-second surveillance video showing a man walking along Indian Creek—a man who police thought might have vital information about the killing in May of Coach's co-owner, Michal Darby. The Kansas City police asked the public for information on June 27, 2017, stating that the person in the video was not considered a suspect in the homicide.

Scott, after his arrest, admitted that he was the man shown in the surveillance video circulated by the Kansas City police department.

Brian Darby says he feels disrespected by the claims of Scott's mother that her son was suffering from paranoid schizophrenia at the time of the murders.

Scott's mother, added that maybe in jail he'd finally get help: "I don't want those demons in him anymore because a person who has never dealt with paranoid schizophrenia — you don't know what it's like. It's hell. Their life is hell."

A lot of people would just as soon not hear that. First, citing a mental illness is seen as making an excuse, which is seen, by many as an affront to the victims and their loved ones.

After the loss of his father and then his father's business, it is quite easy to understand why he would question the motives of Scott's mother in speaking about her son's mental state. Or why he scoffs at the comment that she "says she's hurting just as much as the families of the victims. My father will never get his morning walk again. He'll never see the sun again. He won't get his three meals a day, which her son still has."

In the middle of a rather hot political argument over whether hate crimes from the left are as much a threat as those from the right, conservatives point to this series of unprovoked killings as proof they are correct.

Then there is the pressure from advocates for those who struggle with mental illness. With the ancient stereotype of "all persons with mental illness pose a threat and are dangerous" They are very eager to acknowledge that while the vast majority of those with mental illness are not dangerous, it is possible that sometimes, some mentally ill people do pose a threat.

It is proven however, that racial animus is an obsession, a symptom that only rears its head after the onset of paranoid schizophrenia. The suspect's mother told The Star that her son refused to get treatment for what she has long seen as his paranoid schizophrenia.

This would definitely be a poor defense for Scott, because "not guilty by reason of insanity" is rarely argued and almost never successful. Congress and half the states passed laws limiting the use of this defense. Now, the legal definition of insanity requires a break from reality that is so severe that the accused no longer knows what he is doing is wrong. This standard goes back to the mid-1800s.

Fifth victim: Steven Gibbons, aged 57, was shot in the back of the head as he walked along a south Kansas City street. Video surveillance shows Scott following him off a bus and down a south Kansas City street on August 13, 2017 and he was later seen running from the scene of Gibbons' murder. Gibbons was found in the 1100 block of East 67th Street and he was rushed to the hospital where he survived on life support for over a day before succumbing to his wounds and dying on August 14, 2017.

SCOTT'S COURT APPEARANCE:

A man suspected in five killing on or near south Kansas City trails has appeared in court, providing the victims' families a first chance to see him in person.

Several relatives dabbed their eyes as they left the courtroom. Afterward, Brian Darby, said, "We want justice." Scott is a suspect in the death of Darby's father, 61-year-old Mike Darby, but hasn't been charged in his killing. The police say, at this time, there is not enough evidence to connect and charge Scott with the other three murders.

The Kansas City Star reports that the court appearance Thursday for 22-year-old Fredrick Scott was brief. Prosecutors received a continuance in the case until Oct. 23 over the objections of Scott's public defender. Prosecutors announced last week that Scott had been charged in two killings and is a suspect in three more over nine months. All five were fatally shot, most from behind.

Police say they aren't sure if the murders were racially motivated, but say the accused told detectives he was upset about the 2015 shooting death of his half-brother. The killer was sentenced last week to 45 years in prison.

"Anyone who shoots innocent people walking on a trail should be prosecuted as heavily as possible," Shaton Duncan, who lives near the trail, told CBS affiliate KCTV.

These horrendous murders terrorized the community for months.

"I was in the Army overseas but I didn't want to walk on the trail by myself, that's how dangerous it felt," area resident Chuck Loomis told the station.

It has been an incredibly difficult six months for the family of David Lenox, but news of an arrest has them feeling more confident than ever they'll see justice for their father.

"Yesterday was very emotional with all the families. It was really hard for everyone," said Mindy Lenox.

Lenox and her brother Mike have lived in a true state of pure heartache for the last six months, endlessly working to keep their father's case in the spotlight.

They say while they didn't know exactly what Jackson County Prosecutor Jean Peters Baker would announce Tuesday, the fact investigators suggested Mindy catch a flight from San Francisco to Kansas City tipped them the news was substantial.

Frederick Scott has been charged with two of the murders along the trail - not with David Lenox's - but he is a suspect.

"Now that we have a name and a picture, anyone that knows Frederick Scott that may not have realized that it was vital information for the police," Lenox said. "If they could come forward, that's what we're looking for so that the remaining three families can receive justice as well."

The family says there is some relief just knowing there has been an arrest and that they can rest easier knowing that justice for David Lenox may only be a few tips away.

"I'm so pleased with the Kansas City Missouri Police Department," Michael Lenox said. "I can't thank them enough. Really just tremendous work on their part. They still got more work to do, but I'm very confident they'll get it done."

Since Tuesday's announcement, there have already been multiple tips called in. And anyone who thinks they might have any information at all is encouraged to call the tip line.

It was the Gibbons killing that led police to Scott, who had been mowing lawns to make money and, during the time of the shootings on the trails, had been working at a Burger King at Red Bridge and Holmes roads — within a few miles of three of the shooting scenes.

According to police in Kansas City, Scott did not own a car during the time of the killings, and got around town much of the time by walking. Also, Scott told investigators that he frequently used the Indian Creek Trail as a shortcut. He had a friend at the Willow Creek apartments near the trail. One of the victims was found shot and killed outside those homes. Other than walking, Scott told police that his primary mode of transportation was the public bus.

Allegedly, the bus is where Scott found Steven Gibbons.

Shortly after noon on Aug. 13, police were called to 1146 E. 67th Street, where officers found Gibbons shot in the back of the head.

Detectives found surveillance video that showed Gibbons, minutes before the shooting, boarding a KCATA bus at 75th Street and Troost Avenue. He was followed by a man carrying an iced tea bottle.

When Gibbons stepped off the bus at 67th Street, the man followed him, walking behind Gibbons closing the distance between them.

The surveillance camera panned away from the scene of the shooting, so detectives did not get a video record of the actual murder, but about 40 seconds later, the video showed the suspect running from the shooting scene and boarding a bus again.

Just west of the crime scene, detectives later found an iced tea bottle like the one in the video.

At a nearby gas station, detectives obtained video showing a man buying a bottle of iced tea just a few minutes before boarding the bus behind Gibbons.

Detectives took a still photo from that video and circulated it among police, who four days after the shooting matched the photo to

Scott, whom they found sitting on a wall and smoking a cigarette at 97th Street and Holmes.

Officers watched Scott throw the cigarette butt on the ground and then picked it up, sending it to the department's Regional Crime Lab for forensic testing. That same day, the lab matched the DNA on the cigarette butt to the iced tea bottle.

When police arrested Scott, he allegedly admitted shooting Gibbons but said it had been an accident – that he had been taking the gun out of his pocket when it went off.

While the motive in the killings remains unclear, Scott repeatedly told investigators that he was angry about the 2015 shooting death of his brother, Gerrod H. Woods, aged 23.

Woods was one of two men fatally shot Dec. 14, 2015 during a robbery near East 73rd Street and Wabash Avenue. On Friday, Jimmie Verge, the man convicted in those killings, was handed a 45-year prison sentence.

CONDOLENCES AND RELIEF FOR FAMILIES AND RESIDENTS

Jean Peters Baker said there was no clear motive in the killings. "To the families, there's no motive that makes sense. There just isn't," she said.

John Palmer's family has endured a difficult year since his death a year ago.

He left behind his wife, two grown children, two grandchildren and a large extended collection of family and friends.

Palmer was found shot several times, including in the back, on Aug. 19, 2016, near the Indian Creek Trail. His body had been dragged off the trail into some woods.

Police found a t-shirt at the scene with DNA that matched Scott — who, a year later, under arrest for the Gibbons killing, admitted killing Palmer, a man who relatives said liked to go on long walks through nature.

"He was walking love," said Janelle Kristian of Olathe, Palmer's first cousin. The two grew up in the same house as children. He was, she said, "a man of integrity, honesty and caring."

Palmer wasn't there for the gathering of some 65 people who always celebrate Thanksgiving together, Kristian said. It's been hard "knowing we won't see him again."

But there was solace, she said, when family members began sharing the news from the prosecutor's office, that someone had been arrested and charged.

"I feel glad to think maybe they have found and stopped who was doing this horrible thing," she said. "It's an awful thing to go through."

Kansas City Police Chief Rick Smith said at least 50 law enforcement personnel have worked on the investigation of the killings. The FBI assisted. On Tuesday, Smith said he extended his condolences to the families of the victims.

"We know this has been an incredibly painful and difficult time for each of you," Smith said. "We have worked diligently to bring the person responsible for these crimes to prosecution."

John Sharp, a former Kansas City council member who now leads the South Kansas City Alliance and was at the press conference Tuesday, said people living near the trails could be relieved to know a suspect has been arrested and charged.

"I think it will bring everybody peace of mind," Sharp said. "We had our south Kansas City Alliance problem-solving event on Saturday and a lady told me that how much she missed walking on the trails but her adult children wouldn't let her walk on them anymore.

"I think she wanted me to reassure her it was safe and of course I couldn't do it," he said. "But now I can."

At this point, everyone involved just hopes to continue to collect more tips and more evidence until they can finally solve the other three murders, whether or not that means convicting Scott of them. Were the killings racially motivated? Were they the result of a paranoid schizophrenic who had no professional help with the disease? Either way, they five victims are still gone, forever. We may never know the whole story behind these horrible events, but hopefully, they will be solved and justice will be served.

WEIRD LAND : THE TRUE STORY OF KIDNAPPER FRANKLIN FLOYD

79

CALEY SIMS

Franklin Delano Floyd

Franklin Delano Floyd's life was a long series of strange and tragic occurrences, beginning with the death of his father when Floyd was just a year old. Floyd grew up in an orphanage and turned to a life of crime at a young age, earning himself a lengthy criminal record over his lifetime. By the age of 20, in the year 1963, he was imprisoned for the kidnapping and rape of a 4 year old girl. He escaped from prison, robbed a bank, and then served a ten year prison term.

Floyd was released on parole and soon after committed another crime, attempting to kidnap a woman. He was arrested but posted bail quickly. Floyd then disappeared, spending much of the rest of his life on the run from authorities and using false names to hide his true identity.

However, Floyd's string of disturbing and violent crimes didn't stop. Around the time he disappeared, in 1974, Floyd married a woman in North Carolina. Floyd kidnapped two of the woman's children, including her five year old daughter, Suzanne Sevakis, who came to be known as Sharon Marshall. Floyd raised Marshall as a daughter, though later evidence showed he molested her from a young age. The two moved frequently around the country and used aliases to conceal Floyd's identity.

In the late 1980's, Marshall graduated from high school. A few years later she gave birth to a son named Michael Hughes, who it was later determined was not Floyd's biological son. Soon after, Marshall began working as an exotic dancer. It was during this time, in April of 1989, that Floyd committed the murder of Cheryl Commesso, a fellow dancer at the club where Marshall worked.

Commesso's murder went unsolved for years. Later in 1989, Floyd and Marshall were married. But in 1990, Marshall was killed in a hit and run accident. The driver was never found, and Floyd remains the only suspect in the case to this day. Later that year, Floyd was arrested for the kidnapping he committed in 1973.

Floyd again served a short prison sentence and was released in 1993. But Floyd didn't stop his life of crime. Shortly after serving his time in prison, Floyd attacked another woman. He was arrested for this attack but released on bond. During this time, Floyd went to the elementary school of Michael Hughes, Marshall's son, who had been living with a foster family. He kidnapped Hughes and the school principal, leaving the principal tied to a tree in the woods. The principal was found and survived, but Hughes was never found.

Floyd was finally arrested again in 1994 for the kidnapping of Hughes, though this would be the last time he was incarcerated. In 1995, Commesso's remains were found. The same year, a truck that had belonged to Floyd was found to contain images of child pornography along with pictures of Commesso severely beaten. This evidence was used to convict Floyd of Commesso's murder. In 2002, Floyd was sentenced to death for the murder of Cheryl Commesso and the kidnapping of Michael Hughes.

Early Life

From a very young age, Franklin Delano Floyd led a troubled life. He was born on June 17, 1943 to Thomas H. Floyd and Della Jewel Floyd in the town of Barnsville, Georgia. He had four siblings—a brother Billy and three sisters, Dorothy, Shirley, and Tommye.

In June 1944, when Floyd was just one year old, his father passed away. This left Floyd and his four siblings in the care of his mother, an unstable woman who would go on to have several failed marriages and her own criminal record. In January of 1946, the young Floyd and his siblings were placed in the Georgia Baptist Children's Home by their mother. Floyd's sister Dorothy was later separated from the others and moved to another orphanage in Pinewood, Georgia.

Floyd's mother moved to Florida where she married and subsequently divorced twice. She then married her fourth husband, who she would stay with for the rest of her life. It is unlikely that Floyd ever saw his mother again, though she did visit his sister Dorothy once, a trip that ended with Della being arrested on a drunk and disorderly charge.

In the summer of 1959, when he turned sixteen, Floyd ran away from the children's home he had been living in since he was just two years old. Shortly after running away, Floyd obtained falsified documents claiming he was eighteen years old. He used these papers to join the U.S. Army, using his real name but a fake age.

Floyd's Army career was short-lived, however. He was stationed in Missouri and Oklahoma before his real age was discovered in December of 1959. Upon discovering he was only sixteen, the Army sent Floyd via bus to his sister Dorothy. Dorothy had married since leaving the orphanage and now lived in Gainesville, Georgia. When Floyd arrived, however, Dorothy's husband did not allow him to stay.

A few months later, Floyd began what would ultimately be a life of crime. Early in the morning on February 19, 1960, Floyd broke into a Sears store in Inglewood, California. Police arrived at the scene and Floyd exchanged fire with the police on the roof of the building. He was shot in the back and hospitalized for his injuries at Centinela Hospital.

After recovering somewhat, Floyd was transferred to the prison ward in nearby General Hospital before being sent to the Preston Youth Correctional Facility. His sentence was not long, and by the summer of 1961 Floyd was out on parole. However, in August of 1961 he violated his parole by leaving the country and going on a camping trip in Canada. Floyd was arrested in November of 1961 for this parole violation and was returned to the Preston Youth facility.

A few months later, in January of 1962, Floyd was released. He left California, returning to his home state of Georgia where he briefly lived with his sister Dorothy in Gainesville. He then moved nearer to Atlanta, where Floyd worked at the Atlanta airport for a short period of time. In May of 1962, Floyd moved back to Hapeville, Georgia and lived near the Georgia Baptist Children's Home where he grew up.

It was during this time that Floyd, now nineteen years old, began to commit more horrific crimes.

Kidnapping and Bank Robbery

On May 20, 1962, Floyd kidnapped a four year old girl from a bowling alley in Hapeville, Georgia. Floyd subsequently raped the girl. On July 31, 1962 he was found guilty of child molestation and was sentenced to 20 years in prison. However, Floyd would never serve his full sentence for this crime.

Floyd was sent to Reidsville Prison in Atlanta, Georgia to serve his time. In November of 1962 he was hospitalized at Milledgeville Hospital where he underwent psychiatric testing. Floyd had a number of psychiatric problems, possibly stemming from his difficult childhood spent in an orphanage. His stay at the hospital was lengthy, spanning more than four months.

On March 14, 1963 Floyd escaped from Milledgeville Hospital. Outside the hospital, he stole a car and purchased a pellet pistol. Floyd used these to commit a bank robbery, later claiming he needed to get money to appeal his child molestation conviction. He stole over $6,800 from the Citizens and Southern Bank in Macon, Georgia, and was caught and arrested the same day. Floyd soon confessed to the crime.

On July 12, 1963, Floyd was sentenced to fifteen years in prison for the bank robbery. He was sent to Chillicothe Federal prison in Chillicothe, Ohio. Floyd remained there for several months, though in September of 1963 he attempted to escape by hotwiring a prison fire truck and crashing it into a fence. The escape attempt was unsuccessful.

In October, Floyd was transferred to a prison in Lewisburg, Pennsylvania where he remained until June of 1964, when he was sent to a prison hospital in Springfield, Missouri to be evaluated. Floyd stayed in the hospital for eight months before being transferred to a federal prison in Marion, Illinois.

The prison in Marion was Floyd's longest stay in one facility to that point, and he remained there from February of 1965 until February of

1968. During this time he earned his GED. Floyd's mother also passed away while he was in prison in Marion. In February 1968 Floyd was again transferred, this time back to Reidsville, Georgia. He finished his sentence for child molestation there.

In November 1971, Floyd was sent to a federal prison in Atlanta, Georgia to serve his sentence for his escape attempt in Chillicothe. He was there for another year, and in November 1972, Floyd was released to a halfway house. Soon after, on January 19, 1973 he was paroled.

Just over a week later, on January 27, 1973, Floyd attempted to kidnap a young woman. On February 2nd, he was arrested for the attack. Floyd called a friend he met during his time in prison who bailed him out. After this incident, Floyd disappeared for several years, becoming a fugitive on the run.

Sharon Marshall

Sometime between 1973 and 1975, Franklin Delano Floyd, using an alias, married a North Carolina woman by the name of Sandra Chipman. Chipman had four children, including a baby boy, a five year old girl, and two other daughters. In 1974, Chipman was arrested and served 30 days in jail for writing bad checks. While she was in jail, Floyd took two of her children—the baby boy and the five year old girl—and fled the state. The other two children were placed in a children's home.

When Chipman was released from jail, she was able to reunite with the two children Floyd had left behind. However, Floyd and her other two children were long gone. Chipman attempted to file a report with the police, but she was told that because Floyd was the children's stepfather he had the right to take them.

Chipman's infant son was never seen again, and his whereabouts remain unknown to this day. Her young daughter Suzanne Sevakis, however, remained with Floyd. He gave her several different aliases during her childhood, as he was still a fugitive, but as she grew older the girl went by the name of Sharon Marshall.

In 1975, Floyd got a job working for the Oklahoma school system. In August of 1975, he enrolled Marshall at Wilson Elementary School in Oklahoma. Floyd went by the false name of Trenton Davis while Marshall was enrolled in school as his daughter under the name Suzanne Davis.

In 1978, Floyd had to move again. A babysitter told police that she believed Floyd, or Trenton Davis, was molesting his "daughter". Floyd appeared again in Arizona briefly, where Marshall was again enrolled in school. They didn't stay long, moving to Louisville, Kentucky in 1979.

In 1983, Sharon Marshall began high school. She attended three different schools in 1983 as Floyd moved around, taking her with him. Floyd finally settled in Atlanta, Georgia, assuming the name Warren Marshall. Sharon Marshall enrolled in Forest Park High School, where she was a surprisingly successful student.

Marshall was a smart girl and a good student. By the time she graduated, she had even earned college scholarships for her academic excellence. Not just smart, Marshall was also a popular student. She ran for junior class office and, according to her teachers, was well-liked. She attended a student council leadership conference one summer, where she befriended Jennifer Tanner.

Tanner was later able to give accounts of her friendship with Marshall, shedding light onto Marshall's mysterious life. According to Tanner, Marshall's "father", Floyd, was very strict. She also stated later that Marshall showed her lingerie Floyd had given her. Adding to the strangeness of their relationship, Tanner also said that Floyd was obsessive about Marshall's looks, frequently taking photographs of the teenager.

In 1986, Sharon Marshall graduated high school. She had done well enough to earn a full scholarship to go to Georgia Tech and study aerospace engineering. However, she never went to college and instead stayed with Floyd. Marshall moved to Phoenix, Arizona with Floyd in July 1986. In 1988, Marshall got pregnant. She attempted to run away to Alabama to be with her boyfriend, but he woke up to find her missing one day. She left behind a note saying her father had taken her back with him. Marshall was back with Franklin Delano Floyd.

On March 21, 1988 Marshall gave birth to a baby boy and named him Michael Anthony Hughes. Even after Hughes's birth, Marshall and Floyd continued to move around frequently.

By April of 1989, Marshall and Floyd were living in Tampa, Florida. Marshall was working as an exotic dancer at the Mons Venus club. This is where they met Cheryl Commesso, the woman Floyd was ultimately sentenced to death for killing.

Cheryl Commesso

Cheryl Commesso was a native of the Tampa, Florida area. Just a few years younger than Marshall, she had attended the local Brandon High School, where she participated in extracurricular activities, including singing in the chorus and dancing. Commesso even competed in the Miss Brandon pageant in 1987. Commesso, according to surviving family members, was a bright young girl who just grew up too fast.

In her senior year of high school, Commesso began to run away. She dropped out of school and began dancing at the World Famous Doll House a strip club in Orlando, Florida. Commesso was living fast—she bought a red Corvette and earned enough money dancing to get breast implants. According to her mother, Lois Commesso, she wanted to model for Playboy someday.

In 1989, Commesso was working at the Mons Venus near Tampa, Florida, where she lived with her father. She met and befriended Sharon Marshall who was also working as a dancer at the club.

The friendship turned into a deadly mistake for Commesso. In late March of April 1989, shortly after St. Patrick's Day, Commesso and Marshall got into an argument outside the Mons Venus club. Floyd became involved, accusing Commesso of reporting Marshall for falsely reporting her income, which had resulted in Marshall losing Medicaid coverage for her infant son. According to a coworker of Commesso and Marshall's, Floyd punched Commesso during this argument, leaving a bruise.

Not long after the altercation, Commesso went missing. It was later discovered that Floyd, possibly with Marshall's help, had kidnapped Commesso. Nobody knows exactly where he took her or all the graphic details of what he did to her, but Floyd did leave some clues, whether he meant to or not.

Commesso was last seen by her family a few days before the murder. She was leaving for several days. Commesso packed a bag and told her father she would call him soon, then left, never to be seen alive again. Her car was soon found in the parking lot of the St. Petersburg/ Clearwater airport. This immediately aroused suspicions in her family, who told police that Commesso was very attached to her car and would never have left it.

Commesso's fate remained unknown for years. Finally, in 1995, landscapers found her skeletal remains in a wooded area off of Interstate 275. Medical investigators determined the woman whose skeleton they found, known at the time as "Jane Doe I-25", had been beaten and shot in the back of the head twice. They were also able to identify the body as Commesso's, with evidence suggesting the body had been there for six to seven years, the same amount of time as Commesso had been missing.

Back on the Run

Floyd's other criminal enterprises did not stop during this time. In April of 1989, the very same month that Commesso was murdered, a warrant was placed on Floyd for insurance fraud. Floyd was accused of drilling holes into the bottom of a boat he owned in order to collect insurance money.

Floyd and Marshall were also the primary suspects in Commesso's mysterious disappearance, thanks to the altercation coworkers had witnessed between Floyd and Commesso shortly before she disappeared. Floyd left town soon after murdering Commesso and brought Marshall along with him. The pair left Tampa, Florida in May of 1989 and moved to New Orleans. On June 15, 1989, Floyd and Marshall married, with both the bride and groom using new aliases.

The very next day, June 16, 1989, Floyd's trailer in Tampa burned to the ground. Police ruled that this was intentional arson. Most likely, Floyd was attempting to hide the evidence of Commesso's murder as well as his own identity, as he was still wanted for the 1973 kidnapping case in Atlanta. It appeared that, at least for the moment, Floyd was going to keep running from the law.

Soon after these events, Floyd and Marshall moved again, this time to Tulsa, Oklahoma. In August of 1989, Marshall began working at another adult entertainment nightclub called Passion. She and Floyd would live together in Oklahoma for several months with Marshall working as a dancer. Coworkers say that Marshall was secretive about her past, telling them only that all members of her family were dead.

During her time at Passions, Marshall also confided in some of her coworkers, though she never revealed the truth about her life. She did, however, tell coworkers that she had a new boyfriend whom she had met at the club. Marshall's coworkers claim she was afraid to tell her husband that she wanted to leave him.

Marshall was right to fear what Floyd might do. Less than a year after their marriage in New Orleans, Marshall was killed in a mysterious hit-and-run accident.

Hit-and-Run

On the night of April 25, 1990, the woman who had come to be known as Sharon Marshall was struck by a car while walking on the side of the road to the motel where she was staying in Tulsa. Marshall was hospitalized and survived for five days with her injuries before dying on April 30, 1990. Her funeral was held in Tulsa, Oklahoma on May 4, 1990.

Floyd was a person of interest in the case. He claimed that he was in the motel waiting for her and therefore could not have been the driver in the hit-and-run accident. Floyd was not arrested, though police had their suspicions.

On May 17, 1990, less than two weeks after his mother's death Michael Hughes, Marshall's son, was declared a ward of the state. Hughes was placed in foster care. According to his foster parents, Hughes, who was two years old, was non-verbal and had limited muscle control. His behavior was frequently out of control. Nevertheless, Hughes began to make progress during his time with his foster family.

Identity Revealed

On June 20, 1990, Floyd was finally caught and his true identity as Franklin Delano Floyd was revealed. He was arrested near Augusta, Georgia where he had been living in a trailer, for the 1973 kidnapping attempt he had committed in Atlanta. Floyd was sent to a federal prison in Georgia, and in December of 1990 he was transferred to El Reno Prison in Oklahoma.

Floyd spent a total of 33 months in El Reno Prison. During this time, Michael Hughes's foster parents began the process of adopting Hughes. As part of this process, Hughes's DNA was compared to Floyd's to establish paternity. It was discovered that Floyd was not Hughes's biological father, a fact that would later keep him from gaining custody of Hughes.

On March 30, 1993, Floyd was released to a halfway house. He began working as a maintenance man at an apartment complex. Not long after, he returned to his old ways. On July 4, 1994, Floyd attacked a woman at the apartment complex where he worked. Floyd hid in the bushes of the apartment complex and attempted to attack the woman with a knife when she came home. He was arrested for the attack on August 19, 1994 and was released on bond that same day.

Kidnapping

After he was released from prison, Floyd tried to regain custody of Michael Hughes. However, due to his lengthy criminal record and the recent finding that he had no biological relation to Hughes, a judge denied Floyd's request.

Floyd took matters into his own hands. On September 12, 1994, Floyd went to the elementary school in Choctaw, Oklahoma, where Hughes was in the first grade. Floyd entered the office of Principal James Davis and demanded to see his son. He told Davis he had a gun and showed the gun to Davis, telling him, "If you don't help me, you won't live."

Davis took Floyd to Hughes, and Floyd drove all three of them into the woods in Davis's pickup truck. There, Floyd handcuffed Davis to a tree and left with Hughes.

It's not clear what happened to Hughes after this. Floyd would claim later that Hughes was safe somewhere, then later changed his story and began to say he had killed Hughes.

Floyd returned to Georgia, committing a carjacking in Atlanta. He was also a patient at Grady Memorial Hospital in Atlanta, Georgia from September 21-29, 1994. Floyd didn't stay long, and in October of 1994 Principal Davis's truck was found near the Love Field Airport in Dallas, Texas, suggesting Floyd had been in the area.

Floyd was ultimately apprehended in Louisville, Kentucky. He was arrested on November 10, 1994 at a Kentucky car dealership where he had just started working two days prior. The arrest was for the kidnapping charge, but Floyd would soon be implicated in the murder of Cheryl Commesso.

Putting the Pieces Together

In March of 1995, Cheryl Commesso's body was finally found on the side of I-275 in Tampa, Florida. Meanwhile, the truck that Floyd had stolen when he kidnapped Davis was sold, and the new owner made a disturbing discovery. A thick envelope stuffed with dozens of pictures was found wedged between the bed of the truck and the gas tank.

Some of the pictures showed Cheryl Commesso being tortured and beaten. Others were photographs of Sharon Marshall dating back to when she was a young girl, showing her in sexually suggestive poses. The pictures of Commesso showed her wearing the same jewelry that was found on her body, and there were also pictures of the inside of a trailer and other items that belonged to Floyd. Finally, one picture showed part of someone's thumb. Investigators were able to match the thumb to Floyd. This, along with the photographs of Marshall and Floyd's belongings, was enough evidence to charge Floyd with murder.

On September 28, 2002, Floyd was convicted of first degree murder. The trial had lasted only 90 days and jurors deliberated for just four hours before reaching a guilty verdict. Floyd had an outburst in the courtroom, claiming the prosecutors had framed him and swearing at the judge.

On November 22, 2002, Floyd was sentenced to death. Judge Nancy Moate Ley read the verdict, acknowledging that Floyd had had a difficult childhood, but his long criminal record and the particularly horrific nature of his crime made it necessary for him to be sentenced to death. It was, according to Ley, "not surprising" that the jury had decided on the death penalty.

Floyd is currently on death row in Union Correctional Institution awaiting execution. Many mysteries still surround Franklin Delano Floyd and the crimes he committed. No one has yet been arrested in the hit-and-run accident that killed Sharon Marshall.

In 2014, DNA evidence was used to discover the true identity of Sharon Marshall, linking her to Sandra Chipman. Finally, the truth about Suzanne Sevakis, the North Carolina girl who had been missing for decades, and Sharon Marshall, the mystery girl Floyd had kidnapped, was revealed—they were the same person.

Floyd would also later confess to murdering Michael Hughes, though there is no proof of this claim and no remains have been found. Floyd was able to identify a location in the woods where he claims he killed Hughes. The truth, however, like so many things about Franklin Delano Floyd, may never be known.

SERIAL KILLING STRIPPER: THE TRUE STORY OF ROBYN LINDHOLM

CHELSEA CALBERT
Australia's Most Dangerous Woman

Robyn Lindholm was destined for fame. By the age of 14, this talented, beautiful young woman was already an up-and-comer in the world of Australian figure skating – competing in national ice-skating championships and even performing alongside Olympic legends Torvill and Dean, handpicked by the duo to participate in their sold-out Face The Music world tour.

However, it wasn't her talent on the ice that ensured Lindholm's name would appear on the front page of newspapers for years. Instead, this gorgeous femme fatale will be remembered as a murderer – and potentially, even a serial killer.

The Victorian Supreme Court finally sentenced 43-year-old Lindholm to 25 years in prison for the premeditated murder of her ex-boyfriend, Wayne Amey, in December of 2015 – but then, police began investigating the possibility that Lindholm was behind at least one other death, as well as the possible murder of another past lover.

"She had an uncanny ability to manipulate men," said Chief Crown Prosecutor Gavin Silbert QC, during one of Lindholm's trials.

Always daddy's girl

Born into a wealthy Melbourne family, Lindholm learned at an early age that her good looks and charm could get her anything she wanted. Even her father was powerless to resist. At the age of 11, Lindholm convinced him that she needed a pony. A few years later, a 14-year-old Lindholm demanded pricey skating lessons – and her dad never failed to indulge his daughter's every wish.

While Lindholm relied heavily on her appearance to get ahead, she grew up a fairly hardworking young girl. After excelling at Kilvington Grammar and even at an elite secondary college, Lindholm planned to attend Monash University to study a Bachelor of Science degree. Her love of horses had endured since childhood, and her passion for endurance riding led Lindholm to pursue a career working with animals.

Her bright future began to derail when she accepted a part-time job working in one of the high-roller rooms at the Crown Casino, the Mahogany Room. Even though Lindholm was just a hostess, her long legs and beautiful blonde hair caught the eye of "the Black Prince of Lygon Street." Alphonse Gangitano was an attractive and wealthy underworld crime leader, and Lindholm was unable to resist the allure of the handsome and powerful man's lifestyle of money, sex, and drugs.

Lindholm's demanding nature suited Gangitano just fine. Once again, she was treated like a princess – Gangitano was more than willing to indulge Lindholm's every whim and buy her whatever she desired. When Gangitano was eventually executed in his own home, Lindholm would need to find another way to maintain the intoxicating lifestyle she'd gotten accustomed to – by whatever means necessary.

Simply Irresistible

While working in the Mahogany Room, Lindholm had developed a relationship with Alex Prelac – a regular customer of the exclusive high-roller room who owned the Simply Irresistible Stripping Agency. Lindholm had purchased her first small farm in Glenhope when she was only 23, and agreed to work part-time for Prelac's agency to help pay down her mortgage.

Stripping not only provided Lindholm with a steady income and the exciting lifestyle she was looking for – it also indulged her need to be the centre of attention. Her job with Simply Irresistible wasn't enough, though. Soon, Lindholm made the jump from stripping to working back in Melbourne's underworld as a highly-paid escort, going by the name "Collette."

John Elder, who worked as editor-in-chief of a magazine that routinely hired strippers for pranks and other comical roles, recalled meeting Lindholm when she was only 20 years old – "an ice-skating champion, newly dropped out of a science degree, moving into animal husbandry."

"She talked to me about her dream of owning her own place in the country, horses, a quiet life," he said. "There was nothing to suggest she'd end up burying one, maybe two boyfriends at the wished-for homestead."

Elder added that for Lindholm, stripping was a "means to a real-estate end," and that as soon as she was able to save enough money, she'd move on to her real passion of working with horses.

Soon after she started at the club, Lindholm struck up a close friendship with another stripper, Shari Davison. Davison was an exotic dancer who had previously worked as a circus trapeze artist, and who had just had a baby when she disappeared after leaving the Crown Casino on a Saturday morning in February of 1995. Her body has never been recovered, but investigations soon began to point to her good friend, Lindholm.

"There were so many rumours, ratbags, and depraved offshoots in our digging around," Elder said. "An inquest in 2001 found that Davison had a taste for drugs, booze, and bad men – and was pronounced mysteriously dead."

Apparently, in the weeks leading up to her disappearance, Davison had confessed to some close friends that she was "in serious trouble" with a gang of young Greeks – a gang which included standover man George Teazis, who had recently started seeing a stripper known as "Collette."

Teazis, also known as Templeton, had once been a member of a Richmond-based gang. The gang participated in the trading of weapons and amphetamines, dubbed the "plastic gangsters." Teazis fell head over heels in love with Lindhom, and even went as far to propose to her and move her into his home. However, he vanished in 2005, shortly after the engagement, and his body remains unfound.

A volatile situation

Two weeks prior to his disappearance, Teazis's brother received an upsetting phone call. Teazis was in tears, distraught over having just caught Lindholm in bed with, presumably, Wayne Amey. According to the brother, the couple had a "violent fight," and Teazis decided to leave Lindholm.

On the day Teazis disappeared, Lindholm had been out with a friend. When she came home, she claims the door was open and Teazis was gone. According to Lindholm, Teazis had sent a text at around 2:30am, stating that he was in some kind of trouble and would need a ride home, but she didn't know where he was.

Tearfully, Lindholm took to the press to express her pain and desire to locate her beloved fiancé. In the meantime, though, she moved all the furniture out of Teazis' home and claimed all of his assets – leaving a small box of toys for her fiancé's grief-stricken teenage son, Ross.

"Ross noticed that his father's F100 campervan was missing, along with his motorbike, a boat, a rear-projection television, jewellery, and other assorted goods worth an uncounted tens of thousands of dollars," said Elder. "Ross says he was so stunned at the time, he immediately went to a friend's home to settle himself. Later, he tried calling (Lindholm), to claim his father's belongings."

According to Ross, Lindholm eventually texted to tell him that she'd left some "clothes and his remote-controlled cars" in boxes on the doorstep. When Ross inquired about the vehicles, Lindholm replied that he would be "getting nothing ... and she forwarded her solicitor's details."

And while Lindholm made a show of crying for the press, Teazis' family members claimed that before getting in front of the cameras, Lindholm had been "laughing with her friend." After shedding some tears during the press conference and mourning the disappearance of her lover, she was "seen laughing again when it was over."

She also chose not to mention her new lover to the TV and newspaper reporters. Before Teazis' disappearance, Lindholm had started an affair with a gym owner named Wayne Amey. With Teazis out of the picture and her stripping career taking off, Lindholm was on track to get everything she ever wanted.

Lindholm reluctanty sold her Glenhope farm to purchase land with Amey, a 10-acre property near Bittern. This would give her plenty of space to pursue her lasting love of equestrianism and, eventually, begin breeding horses. Up until her arrest, Lindholm continued to enjoy endurance riding, and at the time Amey was killed, their property was home to eight beautiful – and expensive – Arabian horses.

Lady Macbeth in Lycra

Although Teazis' body was never recovered, Lindholm was formally charged with his murder in June of 2016. In 2005, police had conceded that it was possible that Teazis may not have wanted to ever be found – but since he hadn't used his mobile phone or accessed his bank accounts, they had "grave concerns."

According to police, Lindholm had convinced her new lover, Amey, to help her kill and dispose of her fiancé – a story that was somewhat corroborated by a strip club owner who had hired Amey as a personal trainer.

"He said (Teazis) was knocking Robyn around," she told Elder. "He kept saying he was going to kill (Teazis). It went on and on. It got scary and I stopped training with him."

The charge came just a few months after Lindholm was convicted of persuading another lover, Torsten "Toots" Trabert, to murder Amey. According to Elder, Lindholm and Amey were separating – and Amey had hoped for a settlement that would leave him half of the couple's rural property.

"Lindholm was angry, vengeful, and bitter over the break-up of her relationship with Amey and the loss of the farm, and he became anxious for his own safety," said a newspaper article published in The Sunday Age, discussing the case.

According to defence barrister John Kelly, Lindholm had "lost everything." Unemployed and living out of her car, she decided her only option was to kill Amey – a man she'd once hoped to start a family with.

"Her sense of grievance at the situation she found herself in needs to be viewed through that prism," Kelly told the Supreme Court following Lindholm's plea of guilt. "She had lost all sense of proportion at that stage. But she blamed Amey for the straights she was in because ... she says she had the most wonderful upbringing and childhood she could hope to have."

Kelly added that by 2013, Lindholm was a "40-year-old woman with no prospect that she could see, no means of support, and no property or assets to her name," but added that none of this information "ameliorates what then happened to Amey."

Despite her desire to see Amey killed, Lindholm knew wouldn't be able to commit the murder on her own. If she wanted her ex-lover dead, she'd need to convince her new lover to do the dirty work. While Lindholm considered her relationship with Trabert to be nothing more than a "fling," he had fallen "madly in love."

"Trabert was infatuated with her," said Chief Crown Prosecutor Gavin Silbert QC, noting that the pair were involved in an "intense sexual relationship." He added that Trabert had even left his wife and children to move in with Lindholm – but there was a price to be paid.

"He couldn't keep his hands off her, and the return for her affection was that he kill Wayne Amey," Silbert said. "It was only with the seduction of Travert that she achieved her aims."

According to Silbert, Trabert wasn't Lindholm's first choice. In fact, he told the Victorian Supreme Court during Lindholm's trial that the stripper had attempted to convince several other former lovers to help her get rid of Amey, but Trabert was the first one to agree to her plan.

However, Trabert did need a bit of persuading. Silbert told the court that Lindholm used her sexuality to seduce Trabert into doing her bidding – to the point where, Silbert said, Trabert was completely obsessed with her. Even while locked in a remand cell following his arrest, Trabert sent flowery love notes to "darling" Lindholm.

"I'm missing you so much that I can't sleep because you are not with me ... we are so good together," one note read. "I can't think of my life without. All my love, Toots."

Trabert ended his note with a carefully drawn heart containing the words "I love you forever."

According to plan

The murder was carried out on December 10, 2013 – the day before Amey and Lindholm were due in court to resolve their dispute over a $1.1 million rural property they owned in Bittern. Lindholm directed Trabert and his accomplice, John Anthony Ryan, to attack Amey at his apartment.

The two men beat him repeatedly with a baseball bat, stabbed him, and choked him – and then wrapped him up and stuffed him in the trunk of the car. The group then drove to a remote farm in Mt Korong in Central Victoria, to get rid of Amey's body.

According to court reports, Trabert had tried to find a fourth person to help the trio "finish off" Amey, but this person refused to get involved. At this point, records state, Amey could be heard "begging for his life" from the trunk of the car. When the car was parked at the farm, Trabert and Ryan completed the murder.

"Post-mortem examination revealed that Amey had multiple stab injuries to his chest, fractured ribs, pallor and furrow to the left side of his neck in association with a rope, and multiple lacerations to his scalp," the court records revealed. "The opinion of the forensic pathologist was that Amey's death was a result of one or more of these injuries."

Lindholm kept a watchful eye on her suitor as he and Ryan pushed the body into a crevice between two rocks, ordering them to use more rocks and sticks to cover Amey's corpse and ensure it wouldn't be discovered.

Once the body was sufficiently hidden, Lindholm and Trabert had sex in the bushes, while Ryan went to a nearby Inglewood hotel to meet them for drinks. The trio attempted to use Amey's bank cards to clean out his accounts, and eventually set his vehicle on fire to destroy any remaining evidence.

"(Lindholm) was laughing and carrying on like it was nothing," Ryan told police. "She's on top of the world. They just wanted to f—-ing party, and I just felt ill, ill the whole way."

Charges laid

Lindholm, Trabert, and Ryan were all apprehended by police just days after Amey's murder. A car pursuit between Trabert, Lindholm, and police ended on foot – Trabert was nabbed by police, while Lindholm attempted evade them by crossing a creek. Ryan, meanwhile, was apprehended at a residential address in Coburg after the body was discovered.

"We have found Amey on the top of a hill," said Sen-Constable Philip Gynther, leading homicide detective on the case. "His remains have been place at the bottom of a crevasse between two large rocks. It's been a very long process ... the terrain all looks very similar."

According to court documents, Lindholm pleaded guilty to Amey's murder, while Trabert and Ryan plead their innocence – "each maintaining that it was the other who had killed Amey."

All three received sentences from Supreme Court Justice Lex Lasry – 25 years for Lindholm, 28 years for Trabert, and 31 years for Ryan. According to Lasry, Lindholm had shown "no remorse" for her role in Amey's murder – saying she "no doubt" felt ashamed and embarrassed, but he didn't believe she had a genuine regret for her "bizarre actions" in the "appalling crime."

Lasry also stated the trio had a history of "excessive use" of crystal meth – a drug which tends to fuel "extraordinarily violent criminal behaviour," he said.

While appeals were submitted for reduced terms, Senior Crown prosecutor Douglas Trapnell, QC, said each member of the trio was "equally responsible" for their roles in Amey's murder – whether as an instigator or as a physical killer.

"Because this was a pre-meditated plan and callous killing on the eve of a court hearing, where Amey was to exercise his legal rights, brings it very close to the worst case," Trapnell said. "This man was beaten in the basement of his apartment building where he had the right to feel safe. He was hog-tied … then put in (a car) boot and remained alive for quite some time, albeit with (injuries including) fractured ribs."

Trapnell also argued that the trio had "desecrated" Amey's body by stuffing it into the crevice on Mt Korong, where, without the assistance of Trabert, it might never have been located. Following his apprehension, Trabert had led police to the farm where Amey's body had been hidden.

"The location of the body by my client allowed the family to seek some closure in having the body returned and afforded a proper burial," said Trabert's lawyer, Adam Chernok. "It's arguable it would have been a much more difficult case to prove and indeed may not have obtained the plea of Lindholm."

Chernok added that while Lindholm had a "primary motive" to kill her lover, his client's only motive was "put very simply, your honour, sex."

"If the killing of Amey is Lindholm's wicked design, it is not a truly shared motive in terms of the killing as I've described," Chernok said. "My client is motivated by sex in the context of his particular circumstances."

David Hallowes, who defended Ryan, claimed his client didn't become involved in the plot until after he'd been told that Amey was "mistreating" Lindholm. According to Hallowes, Ryan had believed the plan was only to "beat" Amey – and that without Lindholm's participation, the murder would never have happened.

However, according to Justice Philip Priest, the two men had ample opportunity to back out of the plan while Amey was still alive in the trunk of the car. The fact that they continued with the murder shows "how nasty this killing was."

"Lindholm sought to bring about Amey's murder for two years," stated the judgment from the Court of Appeal in October of 2016, dismissing the bid from the trio. "She tried to persuade others to kill him for her, and eventually, she persuaded Trabert to do it. Trabert and Ryan callously, ruthlessly, and violently carried out her wishes."

In fact, the statement added that Lindholm had continued to arrange for Amey's murder even after she'd broken into his apartment and received a community corrections order. According to court records, Lindholm and others had conducted surveillance on Amey, and she'd broken into the apartment even though she had a swipe card that could have been used to gain entry.

Records show she had told an associate that she'd done this so that "if something happened in the future, it would look like she did not have access to the property."

"It is difficult to overstate Lindholm's moral culpability for this crime," the court said. "She pleaded guilty but the (sentencing) judge found that she was not remorseful. In our view, the sentence imposed on her was a merciful one in the circumstances."

More than sex on legs

Supporting the charges were a series of text messages exchanged between Lindholm and Amey in the weeks leading up to his murder, included as part of the police evidence against Lindholm.

"Look at that ring on your finger Rob," read one message from Amey to Lindholm. "The one I designed, had made and ask you to marry me with, AND I MEANT IT. What better chance could anyone get? You cheated on that ring and me. Remember that when it's on your finger next time you sleep with him."

"Wayne you wouldn't take me back. I tried for months," said one of Lindholm's texts to Amey. "After I recognized my mistakes you still rejected me. I was only good enough to f—k. That was all. When I f—-ked up I was in a bad place lonely and messed up. I know that hurt and I don't know why I did it but the last few months when I begged to come home and I wanted you more than anything you still rejected me continuously. And took everything away."

"I need to feel like I'm more than just sex on legs," she said. "There's Robyn here too not just Collette."

Another text from Amey stated that Lindholm had gotten herself "in this position from a LIFETIME of lies, deception, drug abuse, selfishness and hate."And in another message to Amey, Lindholm told him that if he made her life any more difficult than he already had, "you will regret it Wayne."

According to Lindholm, the couple had been drifting apart for years. By the time their relationship started, Lindholm was in her 30s – ready to get married and start a family. Amey, though, already had a son from a previous relationship and decided to get a vasectomy. According to Amey, the couple "couldn't afford" a child because of their outstanding debts.

By 2009, Lindholm was even more frustrated with her relationship with Amey. He'd promised to retire with her at the Bittern property following his 50th birthday – but that never happened.

"She anticipated that the pair of them would live out there and she would raise her horses out there and they would see out their twilight years together there," said Kelly, Lindholm's lawyer.

Officially, the pair split in 2011, but according to Lindholm, Amey continued to reach out to her for casual sex, right up until his death.

"He was very into that and whenever he got drunk or smashed he used to call me and that was right up until not long ago," Lindholm told police after Amey was killed. "We used to do a lot of threesomes and he used to get me to bring girls home a lot."

However, despite what Ryan had been told about Amey "mistreating" Lindholm, she told police their relationship had never been violent. In fact, she claimed Amey was "kind" to her.

"We loved each other, but we just grew apart," she said. "I would never let anyone hurt (Amey) because he's never hurt me. He was always good to me."

An average guy

According to Amey's teammates from the Camberwell Hockey Club, he was happy, friendly guy – who happened to get in with a "fast crowd." While he wasn't known for sharing many details about his personal life, he had broached the topic of his relationship with Lindholm about three week before he was killed.

Amey had felt as though a weight had been lifted from his shoulders, believing that his dispute with Lindholm over the Bittern property was coming to an end – it was finally on the market, and once the property sold, Amey would be able to get a brand-new start.

"He spoke openly about a breakup some time ago that had turned sour and threatening," said Dugald Jellie, a teammate from the hockey club. "(Amey) was caught in a drama he couldn't undo. He'd tried restraining orders. He wanted only to quit his ex-partner and her friends, sell his country retreat, then one day sell his gym and start anew."

As a youth, Amey had been a top-grade hockey player. As an adult, he'd taken to playing in Camberwell's veteran's squad and working with the club to help develop its younger players. Jellie was one of his hockey mates, who had traveled with Amey to a game in Geelong just a few weeks before he was murdered. He was deeply affected by the news of Amey's death.

"It frightens me to think of (Amey) being hurt and in such peril. It is awful to think of him being so vulnerable, so helpless, so in need of his friends when none of us were there," Jellie said. "I can't stop but think of the moment he was jumped, and of his fears, and how alone he must have felt."

Active investigation

While serving her 25-year sentence for arranging Amey's murder, Lindholm received a new set of charges in June 2016 – naming her responsible for the murder of George Teazis, back in 2005. Appearing before the Melbourne Magistrate's Court via video link from the notorious Dame Phyllis Frost Centre women's prison, Lindholm refused to enter a plea, or speak at all, other than to confirm her name to the magistrate.

In 2017, defence counsel will hold a committal hearing and plan to cross-examine more than 20 witnesses, which will determine if Lindholm will then stand trial.

Investigations are ongoing to determine the extent of Lindholm's possible involvement in the disappearance of Shari Davison, as well.

KILLER SEDUCTRESS

113

GARY RACE

Shayna Hubers

Shayna Hubers is a 21-year-old graduate from Lexington, Kentucky. She grew up in a comfortably middle-class family and was a smart young woman. She graduated from Paul Laurence Dunbar High School in 2009, and went on to college. During high school, Shayna's friends described her as quiet and "most likely to succeed". Shayna graduated from Kentucky's prestigious School of the Arts after making Dean's list in 2012. She was in the process of pursuing a Master's Degree in counseling from Eastern Kentucky University when she took the life of her on-again off-again boyfriend, Ryan Poston and effectively put her life on hold.

Poston was a 29-year-old lawyer and business owner from a successful family of attorneys and executives. He was loved by his friends and family and admired by women. He was known to be friendly, respectful and respectable, and an overall good guy. He met Hubers in 2011 through mutual friends on Facebook and the attraction was instantaneous, as the first photos of Hubers that Poston saw were racy in nature. The two began to chat, and started officially dating shortly after they went on their first date. They continued their relationship for over a year. If it hadn't been for Facebook, the two more than likely never would have met, as Shayna lived 80 miles away from Ryan and had no reason to venture into Ryan's neck of the woods.

Throughout the entirety of the relationship, the couple sent thousands of text messages, including a conversation about possibly taking a two-week long break from each other and the relationship. Hubers was also known to post pictures of herself and Poston on Instagram. The seemingly happy couple exchanged over a thousand photo messages, as well as 20,000 messages through Facebook. Most of the Facebook messages had been sent by Hubers to Poston, who had responded to only a handful of them.

To people who weren't aware of the couple's dynamics, it appeared as if they were a happy couple who had everything going for them. They were both beautiful, successful, and driven. It was a match made in heaven- or so it appeared to be, but the truth was much darker and would become the subject of a complicated trial and a life term in prison.

On October 11, 2012, Hubers and Poston and his family had dinner at the young lawyer's home. After dinner, Hubers went home- she returned a few hours later, however, and the couple got into a heated argument. Poston informed his girlfriend that he wanted to end their 18-month long relationship, and it set Hubers off into a fit of anger. Her anger worsened when she was later told that Poston already had a date lined up with the 2012 Miss Ohio, Audrey Bolte. It's believed that the news of Ryan's new date was what pushed Hubers over the edge.

In the morning, Hubers' mother drove two hours to pick up her daughter and the two went out shopping. They were out for most of the day before Shayna was dropped back off at Ryan's house, telling her mother that she wanted to stay with him. Despite her other asking her numerous times to come home with her, Hubers was adamant that she wanted to stay at Poston's house. Shortly after, Poston became aware that Shayna was planning to stay at his place- he used this time to inform her that he had another date and didn't intend to spend the night with her. By 9 o'clock that night, the young lawyer was dead on his dining room floor.

At 8:53 that chilly Friday night, Hubers placed a 911 call from Poston's condo and said to the responding dispatcher: "Ma'am, I have...I have...I have killed my boyfriend in self-defense".

The dispatcher then asked what happened, to which Hubers replied "He beat me and tried to carry me out of the house and I came back in to get my stuff. He was right in front of me and reached down to grab the gun. I grabbed it out of his hands and pulled the trigger".

The dispatcher then instructed Hubers to step outside with her hands in front of her. Hubers complied, and responding officer, David Fornash's partner cuffed and took her away while Fornash himself went to investigate the crime scene.

Fornash and the other officers who responded to the scene, found Ryan Poston lying on his dining room floor next to a Sig Sauer .380-caliber pistol. The pistol, upon further inspection, was found to have belonged to Poston, who had a passion for guns. "...he would have them in his boot, he would have them in his holster..." says Poston's ex-girlfriend, Lauren Whorley, who claimed that Poston's love of guns made her feel safe.

Fornash went room to room, double checking that there were no other hiding in the apartment and upon finding Poston's body, officers found that he had been shot once in the back, twice in the head, and three times in his upper body. The coroner is called and Fornash sets off for the station where Hubers had been escorted into an interrogation room and sat waiting.

Meanwhile Poston, lying dead on his kitchen floor, was supposed to meet with Audrey Bolte at the Milford Inn bar for a night of drinks and harmless flirting. Poston, however, did not show up and Bolte went home feeling confused. When asked how she felt about him not showing up, Bolte said that it was odd for Poston not to show up or give some sort of notice that he wasn't coming, as he was a very responsible individual.

Friends of Poston claim that he and Hubers were never really in a committed relationship, as Poston lost interest in Hubers rather quickly and made several halfhearted attempts to break it off with her. In fact, by October of 2012, Ryan had made 3 attempts to sever Shayna's ties to him. According to text messages between Poston and his cousin, he was emotionally drained from dealing with Shayna. "I received 75 text messages from her. I am emotionally and mentally spent. I hope she leaves me alone" reads one message between the cousins. Despite this, Poston continued to go out with Hubers and pose for photos.

Shayna, confiding in a friend through text messages, said that Poston had told her that he's only with her because he felt bad when she cries. She is also quoted as saying: "My love has turned to hate."

In one particularly chilling message Shayna claims that "...tonight when I go to the shooting range with Ryan, I want to turn around, shoot, and kill him, and play like it's an accident." The next day, Shayna posts a photo of herself with a gun at the shooting range.

The night of the murder, Shayna was interviewed about the incident. Left alone in the interogation room, Shayne almost seemed proud of what she had done, reports Chief Bill Birkenhauer. He watched her on live camera snapping her fingers, dancing around, and muttering to herself "I killed him, I killed him."

Legally, officers were not allowed to interrogate her without an attorney present, so when she was brought into the interview room they didn't ask any questions. In fact, officers didn't say anything. Shayna, however, readily volunteered her story of how the events took place. She was rambling on for two hours before running out of things to say. According to officers, the men and women who took turns sitting with Shayna, quickly grew tired of her rambling and would have preferred to leave. "Shayna appeared to be nervous, or trying to cover something up" one officer said. "...her stories, after a while, stopped matching up and kept changing." This, according to the officer, might have been happening as a result of Shayna realizing that she was in over her head.

When speaking about Poston's death, Hubers said that she knew he was dead because he was twitching. Her exact words were: "Literally, that's when I knew that he was dead or close to it...the twitching...and that was it." She goes on to explain how she couldn't let him sit there and twitch. She couldn't stand to sit there and watch him die so she shot 5 more rounds into his body to finish him off.

In addition to building a case of self-defense and trying to convince officers that she deeply loved Ryan, she claims that "he was very vain...he wants to get a nose job...I shot him right here-" she pointed to her nose and continued her story "...and I gave him the nose job that he wanted."

Officers didn't buy Shayna's claims of self defense due to lack of evidence that Poston was ever abusive towards her. "She claimed that she was pushed and that he hit her, however, there were no visible marks or wounds at all on any part of Shayna's body" says former FBI profiler James Fitzgerald.

"There was no evidence in Ryan's condo that there was a fight" adds Laura Richards, a prominent criminal behavioral analyst.

Photos from the crime scene show evidence against Shayna's claims of a fight, as there were a number of pill bottles and bullets standing on end on the table. Had a fight taken place, they would have been knocked over or displaced and the murder area would have been left a mess. Instead, it was neat and tidy other than the pool of Ryan's blood that was left behind after the shooting. Shayna had also claimed that Poston had thrown her against a bookshelf. The bookshelf in question, when police arrived, was undisturbed.

As for Shayna's odd behavior when left alone, Richards believes that it was an act in an attempt to appear mentally unstable and open the door for the insanity plea should her self-defense claims fall short. "She couldn't decide which plea to go with- self-defense or insanity. So, she decided to open the doors to both and see which one panned out the best."

After three hours of deliberation, Shayna is charged with one count of first degree murder. In 2014, her trial is well underway and a forensic pathologist mentions that at the time he was shot, Poston had been sitting down- a fact that goes against what Shayna had said previously. According to Richards, this fact alone blows Shayna's claims of self-defense out the window as it shows that Ryan was not charging at her in a fit of rage, as she had previously claimed. Instead, he had been seated and had been seated great distance away from Shayna at the time of the murder. Forensic expert Howard Ryan backs this theory up by going into detail about the shots that Shayna fired at Poston. He says that the first shot was to Poston's head, a fact that is significant due to the lack of blood found on Ryan's shirt.

"If he had been standing up, the gravity would have brought it down...straight down the shirt through the bottom to the pants" he says.

Using the blood stains on the table, Ryan is able to provide further detail as to why he believes that Poston was sitting down. "When she shoots him in the forehead, his head goes down on the table." Poston's head would not have fallen onto the table if he had been in an upright position. From here, Ryan suspects that Poston's back was left exposed, setting him up for the next shot. At the same time that he is being shot a second time, his right arms falls limp and opens up the area of his body that will receive the third shot- which is right underneath of his arm. After this, his body slumps to the floor and remains there until it is removed by the coroner.

Three of Shayna's cellmates testified against her that day, claiming that she had told them that she intended to kill Ryan that night and that he had never been abusive to her. "She laughed about shooting him in the face and giving him the nose job he always wanted" claims Cecily Miller.

Another inmate, Holly Nivens, claims that Shayna made the whole abuse story up. When speaking about the bruises and scratches that Shayna would show people, Nivens claimed that Shayna inflicted them on herself.

Shayna also told her cellmates that she had messed the apartment up and thrown objects around to make it appear as though a vicious fight had taken place.

Shayna didn't take the stand, but prosecutors used her social media and interview footage as a substitution. Despite the overwhelming evidence against Hubers, her defense team maintained its argument that Poston had been abusive and that Shayna had acted out of self defense when she shot him.

A toxicologist was asked to plead in Shayna's defense and said that at the time of his death, Ryan had a strong mix of Xanax and Adderall in his system. He argues that these medications could have caused outbursts of anger and violence, making it possible for Ryan to snap and come after Hubers with a both his fists and then later on, a deadly weapon such as a gun.

A clinical psychologist was also called to testify on her behalf, and he diagnosed her with bipolar disorder with narcissistic tenancies, and post traumatic stress disorder (PTSD).

"She was very distraught. She was depressed" says the psychologist who claims that Shayna had told him that she had suffered from sexual abuse as a child, and was recognized as having alcohol and prescription drug abuse issues.

On the day of the trial, Shayna painted herself as a model girl friend to Poston, claiming that he had been going through a lot and that she had always been there for moral support.

"I was always good to him" she said.

Again, the jury didn't buy the story. Five hours after her trial started, Shayna was officially charged. She appeared back in court three months later for sentencing and was given 40 years behind bars. Shayna's defense team tried to lower the time before she becomes eligible for parole to 8 years instead of 20, but was denied this motion.

Just six months later, her legal team filed another motion seeking a new trial. According to her team, one of the jurors who convicted

Shayna had not been legally eligible to convict her as he was a convicted felon himself. This, according to Kentucky law, made him unable to serve the court and gave Shayna's legal team a reason for a new trial.

It's said that Shayna's new trial date is set for early 2018. Until then, she is behind bars and serving her 40 year sentence as planned.

The new trial was originally set for January of 2018, but has been put on hold for 4 months longer at the request of Shayna's legal team. The extra time, according to her attorney, will be used to prepare.

Despite the 40 year sentence, Ryan's friends and loved ones are left with a sour taste in their mouths. Lauren Whorley, in an interview with a news station, claims that she wishes she would have known what was going on- maybe then she would have been able to help and prevent Ryan from getting too tangled up in Hubers. She also said that she believes the trial should have been handled in an "an eye for an eye" fashion, meaning that what Shayna did to Ryan, should have been done back to her as justice.

"Maybe it's traditional, old-school mentality, but if you kill someone, then you know, it's an eye for an eye. And what you due unto others should be done unto you" she said.

For her, however, the sentencing brought a sliver of much appreciated peace. "I was there when they read it" she said about the final verdict "It was the longest 30 seconds of my life."

Matt Herren, a close friend of Ryan, still struggles to make sense of what went wrong that night. "I think about him everyday," he says "You just don't think something like that will happen to someone you know."

Like Whorley, Matt wonders if there is something he could have done to prevent Ryan from suffering the fate he did. "I know a lot of people in his life feel the same way" he says to "48 Hours" correspondent Peter Van Sant.

Van Sant asked Herren what was lost when Ryan was killed and Herren responded with "He's the type of person you want in your life. Not just a friend, but a loving son, a protective, older brother. He had three younger sisters that he adored." Poston had cared deeply for his three younger sisters and only ever wanted the best for them. In return, they showered him with love and looked up to their older brother.

Ryan and his family had been close-knit, despite his mom and dad divorcing when he was a child. He was close to his father, and when his mother remarried, he grew an attachment to his new step-father, Peter Carter. Ryan thought of him as a second father.

According to Sarah Robinson, a woman who had grown up with Shayna, her future had seemed promising as well. Shayna had been a good student and was never in any trouble.

"I thought she was, close to genius, in my opinion" she said " I mean, she was always in AP classes. Always getting A's in everything."

During her academic career, Hubers had received various awards for academic excellence and leadership.

"She liked to succeed at anything and everything she did" Robinson concludes.

When Van Sant asked her what Shayna had been like with boys in high school, Robinson mentioned that Shayna could be dramatic. "If a guy, broke up with her or something, she would take it pretty hard" she explained "...crying, and a maybe a bit of screaming..she didn't really like to let things go."

When asked if Shayna had been happy with Ryan, Robinson said that as far as she knew, she had been. As far as she knew, they had both been happy.

Ryan's friend, Allie Wagner, claimed that there was something wrong with the relationship from the start when she was asked the same question about Ryan. According to Wagner, Shayna had been cold upon their first meeting. "You could just immediately tell that...that she was obsessed with him," she says.

"He was busy with work..he didn't really have time for anyone" Herren adds. "He didn't want to hurt her feelings..that wasn't the kind of person he was."

As Shayna's denial towards Ryan's disinterest progressed, he started to wonder if he might need to put a restraining order out against her. "This is getting to be restraining order level crazy..." he wrote in a text message to his cousin "She's shown up at my condo 3 times and refuses to leave each time."

Ryan's neighbor, Nikki Carnes claims that there may have been two sides to the tumultuous relationship. She says that Ryan may have been emotionally abusive. According to Carnes, Shayna complained frequently of Ryan putting her down. "She told me that he would say she needed a boob job or a face lift and that she was fat and needed to lose some weight" she says.

Van Sant then asked her why Shayna wouldn't have left and she replied "I guess because she was young and she always told me she loved him." Carnes also told Van Sant that Shayna did everything for Ryan from taking his dog outside to picking up and doing his laundry. On the night of the shooting, she also reportedly heard gunshots but didn't hear the couple fighting, as Shayna had claimed that they had.

Wagner, when asked what she thought could have happened that night replied, "I think she went over there...tried to talk him out of breaking up with her. And I think he just stood his ground for the first time," she said "I think he just said no, like, this isn't working. So she picked up the gun and shot him."

Chief Birkenhauer agreed with Wagner's theory "He wanted to break up with her...I think that Shayna was not gonna be broken up with" he said in an interview with Van Sant.

Prosecutor Michelle Snodgrass explains why Shayna's pleas of abuse were dismissed. "Someone who is in shock does not pirouette," she says in response to the police videos of Shayna singing and dancing in the interview room "Within hours of putting six bullets in Ryan Poston and watching him die, she was dancing and singing."

"There were hundreds of thousands of text messages. And most of them were from Shayna. For every 1 message Ryan sent, she sent probably 50," Snodgrass says "She couldn't stop herself."

According to Snodgrass, rejection was what ultimately pushed Shayna over the edge and drove her to kill the man she so desperately loved.

"Ryan's a bright guy; he's a lawyer" says Van Sant to Snodgrass "Why wouldn't he get a restraining order?"

"Under the law in Kentucky, he didn't qualify for a restraining order. The law in Kentucky required the two to have been living together or to have been married" she replied.

Van Sant then spoke to Hubers' mother, Sharon, about the tragedy. "She graduated cum laude in three years at the University of Kentucky. She was pursuing a Master's Degree in school guidance counseling," she said.

"And what do you want people to know after reading this" Van Sant asked "...in relation to this case?"

"Shayna Hubers is not a child, a girl, a person that would murder someone; that would wake up and say 'OK, I'm going to shoot somebody"

"I want the world to know who Shayna is. And I want them to hear it from her mother" she concludes tearfully.

Hubers and her mother had been close most of Shayna's life, according to Sarah Robinson. "I think she was very close to her mom. I think her mom, for a good portion of her life, could have been her best friend."

This statement is backed up by a quote from Sharon Hubers in her interview with Van Sant: "That child has been a blessing to me. She's my whole life."

"The word that has been used to describe your daughter is evil" Van Sant teold Sharon.

"She's far from evil. Shayna has a heart of gold. She's like her mommy...a loving spirit. That's what I want the world to know" she replied.

After the trial, Shayna spoke up for the first time. Despite having killed their beloved family member, she didn't apologize to Poston's family. Instead, she apologized to her family and friends, and speaks only of herself.

"I'm sorry to my family. And I'm sorry to my friends for letting them down. And I'm sorry for the money my parents had to spend on attorneys" she says, after being convicted of the murder.

"I do wanna help people. I do wanna be something better. And I do want to continue to grow and learn" she said to the judge "And I just don't think a 40 year sentence will help me. I don't think it would benefit me any."

Judge Fred Stine replied to Shayna's statement with his own choice words. "What I think happened in that apartment was little more than cold-blooded murder."

Regardless of what happened that night, a promising young lawyer lays dead, and a successful college student sits rotting behind bars. Two families have been destroyed, and law officials are left baffled. Both the victim and offender have been robbed of their lives- and for what? For a reason that the offender calls love.

* 9 7 9 8 2 2 4 5 6 7 4 7 8 *